F·D·R
at home

DUE

Franklin Delano Roosevelt, photographed by B. Movin-Hermes, 1944.

F·D·R
at home

Nancy A. Fogel, Editor

Dutchess County Historical Society

Published by The Dutchess County Historical Soceity, 549 Main
Street, Poughkeepsie, New York, 12601, and Post Office Box 88,
Poughkeepsie, New York 12602, with the assistance of support from
The Charlotte Cunneen Hackett Charitable Trust, Furthermore, and
The Gannett Foundation.

ISBN 0-944733-00-X

Manufactured in the United States of America.

DESIGN BY BRUCE R. MCPHERSON / BOUND TO LAST

TYPESET IN GARAMOND

FIRST EDITION.

1 3 5 7 9 10 8 6 4 2   2005 2006 2007

Table of Contents

After many years of public service, therefore, my personal thoughts have turned to the day when I could return to civil life. All that is within me cries out to go back to my home on the Hudson River...†

FRANKLIN DELANO ROOSEVELT

† Letter Agreeing to Accept a Nomination for a Fourth Term, 11 July 1944, The Presidential Papers of Franklin D. Roosevelt. All speech citations can be found in the Public Papers and Addresses of Franklin D. Roosevelt.

Foreword

Cynthia M. Koch

Franklin D. Roosevelt's love of Dutchess County is well known. It is equally well known, especially locally, that Dutchess County never loved FDR—that this, the most-elected president in our nation's history, never carried his home county in a presidential election.

This modest volume sets out to change that history. With it the Dutchess County Historical Society not only documents Roosevelt's lifelong love affair with his home in the Hudson Valley; it is also publishing a token of affection, a paean even, to the county's un-favorite son, written (mostly) by those who live in Dutchess County. Unfortunately for FDR's local political legacy, we are sixty years too late.

Though we may not be able to re-elect Roosevelt, the year 2003 is significant nonetheless as the year in which the National Archives and Records Administration, in partnership with the National Park Service and the Franklin and Eleanor Roosevelt Institute, opened a new visitor, education and conference center. In so doing we dedicated the first new building constructed on the Roosevelt Estate since the Presidential Library was opened to the public in 1941. Named in honor of the man who served as Secretary of Agriculture (1933-1940) and vice president during Franklin Roosevelt's third term, the Henry A. Wallace Center offers visitors an array of new and expanded services designed to enhance their experiences at the Franklin D. Roosevelt Presidential Library, the Home of Franklin D. Roosevelt National Historic Site, and surrounding historic venues.

The Wallace Center includes orientation exhibits and a film to welcome the public to the "world of the Roosevelts." The new building offers multipurpose rooms designed for conferences, school groups, and special programs. It includes a café, state-of-the-art audio-visual facilities, a 140-seat auditorium and a museum store. The architectural design of the new center is based upon the simple lines of early Dutch buildings in the Hudson River Valley. FDR loved that style of architecture and designed his Presidential Library to reflect colonial Dutch influence.

Simultaneously, the original Library building was renovated to create a new 3,000 square foot special gallery. That gallery, named for long-time president and chairman of the Franklin and Eleanor Roosevelt Institute, William J. vanden Heuvel, features a schedule of exciting exhibitions drawn from public and private collections worldwide as well as traveling exhibits from the nation's top museums.

This volume is planned as a commemoration as well as a celebration of these exciting new additions to the Roosevelt Library and Historic Site. It is a fitting way to begin to show the world the wealth of new material on the Roosevelts that will be the subject of lectures, educational programs, conferences and exhibits that the new facilities are making possible. It is therefore wonderfully appropriate that the Dutchess County Historical Society conceived this book as a way of bringing to light Roosevelt and his neighbors and the people he knew in Dutchess County. I suspect it would have pleased Roosevelt. He was a founder and supporter of the Dutchess County Historical Society—so much so that he set aside a room for the Society as he planned his Library in the late 1930s.

The editors charged the authors whose work is assembled here with the task of helping people come to know Roosevelt as a local citizen: the town historian and warden at St. James Church in Hyde Park, who concerned himself with the schools, post offices, roads, architecture, and rural nature of the Hudson Valley, even as he led the nation and world to meet the greatest crises of the twentieth century. This book is emphatically not about the New Deal or World War II. It is about Roosevelt at home, with his neighbors, his hobbies and his heritage.

The subjects are wide-ranging—from FDR the birder, tree farmer, historic preservationist and amateur architect, to the scion of one of the great Hudson River families; this volume allows us to engage with personal reminiscences and stories of FDR and his commitment and support of local institutions, government, clubs and communities.

This book is also not about politics—despite the two articles dedicated to a critical campaign, but FDR being FDR, the subject is never far from the surface. And, it is precisely because of his enormous capacity to engage—with people, ideas, and actions—that this glimpse of the private man so richly illumines our understanding of the public Roosevelt. In leading the nation, Roosevelt's private side was very much a part of the public man. Whether he was speaking to farmers in Georgia or addressing a national radio audience—say on Constitution Day—or at a press conference on cherry trees and the Jefferson Memorial, FDR simply could not resist drawing upon his Dutchess County roots.[1] And, of course, when in Dutchess County, the temptation was even greater. In speeches given before local audiences his neighbors learned about his family roots in the colonial history of Rhinebeck and Kingston, the story of "Kansas" in the Town of Clinton, or recollections of the first electric lights and muddy streets in Poughkeepsie.[2] He drew on his love of history, his love of his home, of farming and architecture, and unabashedly used these devices to make himself everybody's "neighbor."

He literally and figuratively welcomed the world to his doorstep. He made Lend-Lease an analogy for neighborliness among nations and he hosted royals from Britain, Norway, Greece and the Netherlands "family-style" at Springwood. He was as likely to invite Winston Churchill to his home as he was to host the Hyde Park School Board. For a time in the late 1940s Hyde Park seemed so much the center of world affairs that it was considered as a home for the United Nations.

While FDR introduced Hyde Park to the world, he also bequeathed to his beloved Dutchess County a rich heritage that includes beautiful public buildings, schools, a National Park centered on his Home, a Presidential Library and Museum, and great preserves of open space. In these gifts he gave us enduring and very personal things. In his will he bequeathed to the American people his family home, the first president to invite all of us to own his legacy, literally. In conceiving the first presidential library, he gave the gift of knowledge so necessary to a democracy. Drawing upon Alfred North Whitehead's characterization of the university as a place for the creation of the future, Roosevelt described the Library's purpose as the place where all citizens would come "so to learn from the past that they could gain in judgment for the creation of the future."[3] We live a future that in countless ways is shaped by the policies, programs, and personality of this one great man. I hope you enjoy our book.

Cynthia M. Koch, Director
Franklin D. Roosevelt Presidential Library and Museum
Hyde Park, New York
September 2003

NOTES

1. Franklin Roosevelt referred to Dutchess County in his "Remarks to the Master Farmers Groups" on 25 October 1935; "Radio Address on Constitution Day" on 17 September 1938 at Washington, DC; and "Press Conference" on 18 November 1938 at Washington, DC.

2. Franklin Roosevelt referred to Dutchess County in his "Remarks at Welcome Home Party" on 30 August 1934 at Hyde Park, NY, and his "Remarks at Poughkeepsie" delivered on 2 November 1936 at Poughkeepsie, NY. Locals referred to an area north of Clinton as "Kansas," but no one knew why they called it that. Franklin Roosevelt researched the origin of the name and discovered that around 1850 agents living in the Territory (later the State) of Kansas came to Clinton to recruit new settlers. Six or eight poor families boarded up their farms and left on a train bound for the West.

3. Roosevelt, "Remarks at the Dedication of the Franklin D. Roosevelt Library at Hyde Park, New York," 30 June 1941.

F.D.R. and His "Neighbors"

F. Kennon Moody

In July 1940, Franklin D. Roosevelt had just been nominated as the Democratic candidate to run for a third term as President of the United States of America. On the 24th of that month he drove to the small Dutchess County hamlet of Salt Point to speak with Hardy Steeholm, a Justice of the Peace there. As the judge later told the story, FDR spoke: "I came here first of all as a neighbor and to talk a little politics."[1] From his days as a fledging New York State Senator, to his last tragic days as President, FDR carried a perception of neighbors that had a profound effect on his pursuit of politics. In hundreds of speeches and radio broadcasts the voting public heard him speak of his "friends" and "neighbors" with such a unique and inimitable pronunciation of the words that their use became a characteristic almost totally identifiable with the political life of Franklin D. Roosevelt. So total was the identification of Roosevelt with these phrases that a prominent historian, writing after FDR's death, would claim that "Roosevelt could say 'my old friend' in eleven languages."[2]

FDR habitually referred to the residents of Dutchess County as his "neighbors," a prime word in his social and political vocabulary. In 1910, as he conducted his first political campaign, he was not very well known in Dutchess County but he was already using

Ken Moody is an educator and past Dean of Students at Dutchess Community College, Poughkeepsie, NY. As an adjunct professor he has taught courses in American History, Western Civilization, Sociology, Religion and Behavioral Science. He currently is a consultant on research at the Franklin Delano Roosevelt Library in Hyde Park, NY.

the phrase, "my friends."[3] As he left the dreary practice of law in New York City to assume the excitement of political life, these early "friends" of 1910 quickly became part of that larger group he referred to as "neighbors," a group that quickly grew to include the entire population of Dutchess County.

By the time he had become the Assistant Secretary of the Navy he was convinced that he had always lived in Hyde Park, glossing over the fact that he had a home in New York City, a summer home in Campobello, and would occupy rental houses in Albany and Washington, D.C., from 1913 to 1921. As Vice President of the State Forestry Association of New York, he was listed on the letterhead as a resident of New York City. His comments to F. F. Moon, at Syracuse University, reveal just how complete the transition had been:

> By the way, I wish you would change my address on the Association's letter paper to Hyde Park, Dutchess County, New York, as I never have been and hope I never will be a resident of New York City.[4]

The residents of Dutchess County had entered into a unique relationship with FDR. Through an unsuccessful campaign for Vice President, two successful campaigns for the Governor of New York State, and four successful campaigns for the Presidency of the United States, the residents of Dutchess County were to be known and dealt with by Franklin. D. Roosevelt as his "neighbors."

After he had been nominated for the Vice Presidency on the 1920 ticket with James Cox of Ohio, he turned to the place that represented the source of his inner strength that had, and would enable him to meet and overcome the trials of political life—the rambling estate known as "Springwood," and the quiet village of Hyde Park. Springwood would always represent his inner political gyroscope, from whence he gained his political balance. After a parade along the Albany Post Road, the crowd gathered at Springwood—Roosevelt accompanied by John E. Mack and Tom Lynch. His next-door neighbor, Senator Newbold, called him "our Hyde Park boy" and received a rousing cheer. At the end, Roosevelt spoke to cement this relationship to the citizens of Dutchess County:

> Neighbors, I am moved more by this than by anything else in my life…. I want to tell you from the bottom of my heart that my success is due to my association with the good old stock of Dutchess County and the straight-thinking people I have been brought up among here.[5]

Twenty years later, following his election to a third term, he still spoke to his neighbors. He was quoted on the front page of the *Poughkeepsie Eagle News*:

> You've got another four years in which to know your neighbor is living in it [the White House], but I can tell you I'd much rather live here [in Dutchess County].[6]

Even his extemporaneous remarks on the campaign trail reflected his self-perceived relationships. Speaking in Beacon on November 7, 1932, he reminded his listeners:

> …a lot of water has gone over the dam since then (1910), but I am still living in Dutchess County, you are still my neighbors, and no matter what happens tomorrow I am still going to be your neighbor and I am still going to live in Dutchess County.[7]

And on his fourth and final election eve, FDR was still greeting his neighbors in the manner of that first rally in 1920:

> The President sent word to Elmer Van Wagner, Chairman, Democratic Committee, Hyde Park, that at 11:00 o'clock… he would receive the Hyde Park neighbors as usual. And they, in time, greater numbers too, than in 1940.[8]

In 1927 Ferdinand Hoyt purchased the *Beacon Standard*, a weekly newspaper in southern Dutchess County. He approached his friend and neighbor, Franklin D. Roosevelt, with a proposal that FDR write a series of columns. The July 16, 1928 issue announced:

"Franklin D. Roosevelt to Write Special Weekly Article for Readers of the *Standard*." The first column appeared on August 2, 1928, entitled "Between Neighbors," and was addressed "to my neighbors in Dutchess County."

The election of 1928 started a trend in voting in Dutchess County that would continue throughout FDR's political career. In all the presidential elections, Franklin Roosevelt won not only the majority of the votes of the Electoral College but also the majority of the popular votes cast. In none, however, did he carry Dutchess County or his hometown of Hyde Park. Such results led Ferdinand Hoyt to lash out editorially: "Dutchess County should be ashamed of Hyde Park…. Beacon…gave the candidate for Governor a much better demonstration of neighborliness."[9]

His neighbors helped define the man. Franklin D. Roosevelt was not only the intense young state senator fighting the Tammany Hall political machine over the nomination of "Blue-Eyed Billy" Sheehan, or the brilliant young politician struck down in his prime with crippling poliomyelitis, or the American Moses leading his people through the devastating wilderness of the Depression years, or the heroic allied wartime leader fighting the scourge of the Axis powers. He was also a man who defined himself with his relationships to the aristocrats of the Hudson River Valley, the tradesmen of Hyde Park, and the residents of the upstate County of Dutchess. He was a man of global fame and immense power who was infinitely complex and to many persons almost incomprehensible. Existing in the two worlds of global politics and small town values, FDR has been most often studied and analyzed as if he existed only in a framework of national and international activity. Too often his relationships to the insular and sometimes warped world of Dutchess County have been ignored in favor of the more inclusive global frame of reference. Such an approach has severely limited the portrait of Franklin D. Roosevelt presented to the public. In order to understand some of the complexity of the man and the myth, he must be seen in relationship to the time, the place and the people, all of which provided his roots.

His "neighbors" could be divided into three distinct groups: 1) members of the aristocracy who also lived on estates along the east bank of the Hudson River; 2) residents of the Town of Hyde Park; and 3) residents of Dutchess County, who lived outside the Town of Hyde Park.

Who were these neighbors, the aristocratic River Families that formed the social structure in the Hudson Valley in which the Roosevelts participated? A few were recognizable by the general public—Levi P. Morton, Lewis Stuyvesant Chandler, Franklin Hughes Delano, Franklin Roosevelt, Vincent Astor, Frederick Vanderbilt. However, most were not recognizable to the average American citizens of the late nineteenth and early twentieth centuries: Archibald Rogers, William Dinsmore, Jacob Ruppert, Thomas Newbold, Samuel Huntington, Tracy Dows, Thomas Suckley. To list the names is not enough. These were not merely families that visited in each other's homes, attended dances and receptions that marked the passing of each year's holidays, or who sought out familiar names for business ventures. They were the last practitioners of a lifestyle that was perhaps unique in the United States in the latter nineteenth century. It was a lifestyle that was rustic but elegant, luxurious but not ostentatious. A guide on a Dutchess County Historical Society tour in 1918 described the River Family way of life in words that might well have been used by any member of the that elite group to describe their existence:

> This is a region, which, to me, is set apart from the rest of
> the universe. In other places one may agreeably live, but I
> am convinced there is here an amenity not elsewhere to be
> found.[10]

The River Families were approximately forty-five to fifty in number. For about twenty-five miles, from the estate of "Woodcliff" on the southern boundary to the estate of "Northwood" at the northern boundary, a series of country estates dotted the eastern bluffs of the Hudson River. The roots of most of these families had grown on this shore of the Hudson since the early days of the nation.

Most of the families could trace some relationship to the Livingston family—Judge Robert Livingston was residing at Clermont at the beginning of the Revolution. At his death the Livingstons owned 240,000 acres in the Catskills, 17,000 acres at Clermont, the Beekman Patent and various parcels in Dutchess County. Eleanor Roosevelt would be a descendant of the Livingstons.

As the Roosevelts established Springwood, other estates surrounding Hyde Park and northern Dutchess County were also prominent. The neighbors are often mentioned in the Roosevelt Papers. Franklin's father, James, was a breeder of Alderney cattle, as was William Dinsmore. Franklin's uncle and aunt, John and Ellen Roosevelt, lived at Rosedale just south of Springwood, while his half-brother, James Roosevelt Roosevelt, and his wife lived just next door at the Red House.

Franklin played as a child with Edmund Rogers and Mary Newbold. Holiday parties and dances were common affairs at the home of Colonel and Mrs. Archibald Rogers. Sara Delano Roosevelt mentions many of the families in her diaries:[11]

> Dec. 11, 1881 – Mrs. Lewis Livingston
> Feb. 7, 1882 – Mr. & Mrs. William Dinsmore
> Sept. 20, 1901 – Mr. & Mrs. Archibald Rogers and the Newbolds
> May 21, 1916 – The Vanderbilts.

The River Families were wealthy, with roots sunk deep in the soil of the eastern bank of the Hudson River. The first generation of estates derived their financial foundation from the land; by the second and third generations, income from the land was insufficient to support the estates. In the latter part of the 19th century the estates found their financial base elsewhere—in banking (Thomas Suckley), in real estate (William and Vincent Astor), in transportation (James Roosevelt), investing (Archibald Rogers), and in finance (Franklin Delano). The change in the financial support of the estates also changed the character of estate living.

Although the estates still had complexes of outbuildings and

Left: FDR at the age of 7 with friend Edmund Rogers, Hyde Park 1889. *Right:* Mary Newbold, FDR, Muriel D. Robbins and "Tip." FDR PRESIDENTIAL LIBRARY.

farming operations, these became adjunct activities guided by the gentlemen farmers, the English country squires who earned most of their living in New York City. James Roosevelt was one of the few to have a farming operation that paid its way in the early years of his residency at Springwood. For many of these families, the estates were only one among many family dwellings. The James Roosevelts kept an apartment at the Hotel Renaissance, West 43rd Street, New York City. The Archibald Rogers family was perhaps the only River Family that lived year-round on their estate, "Crumwold." The *Poughkeepsie Sunday Courier,* of 19 January 1913, noted the migration from country estates to city dwellings:

> Mr. & Mrs. Archibald Rogers, Mr. & Mrs. Frederick W. Vanderbilt, Mr. T. Howard and family, Mrs. James Roosevelt, the family of Senator Franklin D. Roosevelt, Hon. Thomas Newbold and family, all of Hyde Park, are now in town for the winter. Most of the above-mentioned, however, keep their country houses open and spend the weekend in Hyde Park.[12]

Since the estates were so distantly situated from their financial bases, the life on them sometimes assumed an air of a life of leisure. They were isolated from the world of business. For many of the estate residents it must have seemed that life was composed of ice-boating on the Hudson, sledding on the broad lawns, horseback riding through the woods, and various types of social gatherings in each others' magnificent homes. An article in the *Sunday Courier*, 7 January 1900, noted "Mr. and Mrs. James Roosevelt gave a German (party) at their home in Hyde Park…in honor of their son Franklin…." An article of 9 June 1912, showed pictures of the wedding of Ellen H. Rogers with guests who included Senator Elihu Root, Mrs. U.S. Grant, Senator Henry A. Dupont.[13]

In 1936 the estates once again reached a point of great change. Martha Collins Baynes, in a sociological study of Hyde Park, noted: "nearly all of the Hyde Park estates are for sale but are unlikely to be bought, since taxes on such properties are high."[14] The homes of the River Families had played such an important role in his growing years that FDR sought to save some of them. When Glenburn, the home of the Dow family was for sale he wrote to a friend in New York City: "Can't you run around to find a millionaire to buy it?"[15] He tried to save others—Crumwold and Ferncliff—but his success in saving the estates was only slight. The Vanderbilt Mansion, Springwood and Bellefield are currently owned by the Federal Government. Three others—The Point, Mills Mansion, and Clermont are owned by the State of New York.

From his earliest childhood days of playing with the children at Crumwold and Bellefield, to his last dark days of illness and death at Warm Springs he shared the company of various members of the neighboring River Families, people who were like him. On his final day, April 12, 1945, as he sat posing for a portrait, two of his neighbors (who were also distant cousins) were there—Margaret Suckley was crocheting while Laura Astor filled vases with flowers.[16]

Residents of the Town of Hyde Park were surely included among FDR's "neighbors." Many of them lived their entire lives in the shadows cast by the members of the River Families. To live in a setting whose primary identification among most Americans is as the home of the wealthy (the Vanderbilts), or the home of the famous (the Roosevelts) surely was often a trial for the residents of Hyde Park. Many must have thought they were merely props to be utilized as the media wrote of their more famous citizens. A *New York Times* reporter once journeyed to the wilderness of Hyde Park and wrote:[17]

> The crowd was both urban and suburban. Farmers and their families in homespun and city folks in the smartest of fall fashions rubbed elbows and united in their applause for both candidates [Roosevelt and Lehman].

These particular Roosevelt "neighbors" became indignant and replied:

> The reporter must have had an idea that he was visiting in the Ozarks or the mountains of eastern Tennessee. Perhaps he was trying to delight his employers…by giving his readers the notion that Mr. Roosevelt was vastly democratic—just a good fellow—to attend a gathering of primitive ruralities. It's a wonder he didn't make the girls barefooted and the boys in squirrel caps."[18]

Hyde Park was more than a stage setting. It was home for Franklin Roosevelt. It was here he had been born on a wintry day, January 30, 1882. And it was to Hyde Park he returned on a spring day in April 1945, to be buried in his hometown. No clear understanding of FDR and his relationship to Dutchess County, or the world, can be gained without exploring his relationship to Hyde Park and its citizens, his "adjacent neighbors." Eventually the words "Hyde Park" became synonymous with the initials FDR. To speak of one was to evoke the spirit of the other. FDR drew his value primarily from the land and from his ancestors—both were located for generations in the Town of Hyde Park.

Here his ancestors had lived their lives in quiet rural splendor and it was here that FDR over the years purchased many additional acres. Ultimately, it was the people of Hyde Park who helped to broaden his perceptions about society even as he was helping them to realize and accept their responsibility for the well-being of his other friends and neighbors.

The residents of Hyde Park had been present throughout his life. They were his playmates in childhood (Edmund Rogers and Mary Newbold). They were his political cronies (Morgan Hoyt and Thomas Kilmer) in adulthood. They were his fellow church members (Edmund Morgan and Thomas Newbold). They were his fellow devotees of local history (Benjamin Haviland). FDR was involved throughout his life with organizations in Hyde Park. The longest of his associations was with the St. James Episcopal Church, an association that began on Sunday morning, March 20, 1882, with his christening in the St. James Chapel by the Rev. Philander K. Cady.

FDR's father, James, had been a vestry member at St. James in 1858, and later served as the Senior Warden of the vestry until his death in 1900. His son, FDR, was to follow in his father's footsteps, becoming a member of the vestry in 1906, then Junior Warden, and finally Senior Warden until his death in 1945. Even as his life became increasingly complex and busy, FDR continued to be an active member of the St. James Vestry. During his battle with poliomyelitis the vestry meetings often were held at Springwood.[19]

The meetings of the vestry at Springwood illustrate an important and revealing fact about his relationships to the residents of Hyde Park, and to people in general. He was unique among leaders in that he controlled situations in which he met and dealt with people. This grew to be an important social and political tool as he remade his life in the 1920s. Letters and memoranda flowed from Springwood in the twenties. Many of these were to Hyde Park residents and related to town affairs.

One of the major concerns of the members of St. James Vestry was to keep the parish on a sound financial base. The events of October 1929 serve as an example of the problems often faced by the vestry. On October 4, 1929, FDR (the Senior Warden) received a letter from Edmund P. Rogers (the Junior Warden), expressing concern for the deficit at St. James for 1929. He proposed that the church treasurer, Les Bilyou, and others were to raise $200 from the "villagers." He and FDR would contact names on the enclosed list in an attempt to raise $1,500, which, in turn, would be matched dollar-by-dollar by Mr. Vanderbilt.[20] FDR was assigned several families including the various Roosevelts (Mrs. James, Mrs. J.R.), the Newbolds, Rogers, Mills, and Dinsmores. The drive was successful.

As the church of the President and the River Families, the paternalistic, and/or proprietary feelings of some of the wealthy members was sometimes a burden. Edmund Rogers, at one point asked FDR to check up on the church treasurer—"…to keep a closer tag on how he is running the church finances…. You must remember that he is nothing but a village drug store clerk and while perfectly honest, he is not very familiar with banking affairs.[21]

Of all his non-political activities—farming, manuscript collecting, record publishing, church affairs, etc.,—surely his most continuing involvement with the residents of Hyde Park, was with the school system. His interest in the schools had its roots in the land and his family. Nowhere did he express it more clearly than at a teachers' conference in the Franklin D. Roosevelt High School in Hyde Park on October 5, 1940:

> …back in 1870 my father had helped, with very great pride, to build the red brick school over in the village, where it still stands, and it was considered a model in its day.[22]

Even if a family tradition, FDR's involvement was not just honorary in nature. As early as his second term in the State Senate, he was corresponding with a resident concerning the school curriculum. Mr. E. D. Mueser had written to advocate a plan, which would emphasize more vocational studies in the district curriculum. FDR replied that he was in favor of such a plan and that he did "appreciate how necessary it is that the weak schools should be consolidated and that the courses of study should be made to suit more closely the needs of the district where the school is located."[23] Most of FDR's school correspondence did not discuss curriculum but dealt with issues like over-crowding and by implication the need for further school building.

In 1937 Maude Smith Rundall, a district supervisor, authored a "Survey of Educational Needs and Opportunities in the Town of Hyde Park, Dutchess County, New York."[24] Centralization and the building of new schools were proposed. Once again a meeting was held at Springwood to discuss the findings, and a proposal was made to attempt to secure a federal grant through the Public Works Administration. In the fall of 1938 voters cast their votes in favor of centralization and a bond issue.

The school building issue provided a tangible example of how the needs of the varied categories of FDR's "neighbors" sometimes became intertwined to the point of conflict. FDR's neighbors in Hyde Park needed and wanted a school, which he supported. FDR wanted it to be built of fieldstone. A letter from Reeve Palmer, representative of the Bricklayers and Plasterers Union #44, American Federation of Labor wrote to the president:

> If these buildings are constructed of field stone it means that…stone masons from different parts of the state and perhaps from outside the state would be used…please reconsider your pleas for field stone…[25]

FDR continued to be closely involved with the schools, even to the point of complaining that Arthur Halpin was asking an excessive amount (one percent of the total costs) to provide the legal work for the school construction. Being the President, he complained directly to Harold Ickes, administrator of the W.P.A, saying that Halpin was demanding an excessive amount. Thinking that his fellow vestryman was jeopardizing the school grant, FDR wrote to E.K. Burlew, First Assistant Secretary, Department of the Interior:

> …I think you should pass the word down the line this silly business on the part of Brother Halpin has got to stop.[26]

Roosevelt's most famous tenant and a favorite source of understanding concerning his Hyde Park neighbors was Moses Smith. Without FDR's permission, Moses Smith lobbied to have the high school named after the President and was successful.

> At a recent meeting of the Centralized School Board of Hyde Park, I am informed that the Junior-Senior High School at East Park was named the Franklin D. Roosevelt—which I have worked pretty hard for, hoping this will meet with your approval.[27]

In 1929 a group of Hyde Park residents formed the "Roosevelt Home Club," to act as a "non-partisan" vehicle designed to promote the political interests of FDR. By 1932 the club had grown to a total of 492 members who occasionally met at St. James Parish Hall. They also sponsored the annual "Home Coming" gathering held from 1934-1940 in August of each year at Woodlawns, the home of Moses Smith (located on the west side of Rt. 9-G just north of the intersection of 9-G and Creek Road).

> We are not a political club in the last analysis. This is a gathering of a lot of neighbors in this and adjoining townships who come here every year to get acquainted again.[28]

After many years of having the President for a neighbor, the time came for Hyde Park to have a new post office. FDR was very involved in the new federal building in his hometown. The new building was to be built with fieldstone and decorated inside with murals. FDR was so involved that he even found the fieldstone at no charge and told the General Services Administration where it could be found.

> When you come to the building of the new Hyde Park post office please make a memorandum that Mrs. Walter Graeme Elio, 520 E. 87th Street, New York City, has offered free of charge, the stone walls on the hundred acre farm owned by her at the entrance to the Mill Road, just east of the Hyde Park village.[29]

He also wrote to the Works Project Administration: "I hope you will give him [Olin Dows] the commission [to do the murals]…." on behalf of his River Family neighbor, artist Olin Dows.[30] To these Hyde Park neighbors he had given the opportunity to vicariously participate in the life of the larger nation. From these neighbors he had learned the methods of communicating with the ordinary masses that would enable him to become a master at communicating with the nameless citizens across the breadth of the United States. When his magnificent voice filled the airwaves, it was of his local Hyde Park neighbors that he was often thinking.

Had the German forces taken all of Roosevelt's wartime communications at face value, they would have arrived at the conclusion that the American and British war efforts were being directed by FDR's neighbors in Hyde Park. In a series of wartime cables between Roosevelt and Harry Hopkins, the two contrived code names for their own private use. Many of the World War II allied leaders were baptized with the names of Hyde Park residents. General George Marshall, Army Chief of Staff, was "Plog" [the superintendent of Mrs. James Roosevelt's estate]; Sir Winston Churchill was "Moses Smith" [A Roosevelt tenant farmer]; General Dwight Eisenhower was "Keuren" [estate worker with Plog]; Sir Stafford Cripps was "Mrs. Johansen" [the owner/operator of a gas station/restaurant near Val-Kill]; General Carl Spaatz was "Depew" [Mrs. James Roosevelt's chauffeur]; Sir Charles Portal, British Chief of the Air Staff, was "Rev. Wilson" [Rector of St. James Church]; Sir Alan Brooke, Chief of the Imperial General Staff was "Mr. Bee" [Christian Bie was the caretaker at FDR.'s Top Cottage]. Thus, even in the midst of a complicated conflict, the giving of such code names symbolically stated that a group of neighbors had joined together to provide for the common good and to pursue the common welfare.[31]

Franklin D. Roosevelt was a man who had lived a life full of abrupt changes—from a few childhood friends to the enforced camaraderie of a prep school, from health to a devastating sickness, from a bedridden recuperative young man to a successful politician. But the greatest change occurred when he left the quiet life of a private citizen and the solitude of Springwood to partake in the excitement of political life as a public figure. One afternoon in 1933, on the campus of Vassar College he recalled that change:

> I chanced to be in Poughkeepsie on a Saturday…in front of the courthouse I ran across a group of friends of mine. As I remember, they were Judge Morschauser, George Spratt, John Mack and Judge Arnold…. they took me out to the policeman's picnic in Fairview. On that joyous occasion of clams and sauerkraut and real beer I made my first speech and I have been apologizing for it every since…. And also on that same occasion I started to make the acquaintance of that part of the county that lies outside the town of Hyde Park.[32]

At the young age of twenty-eight FDR had finally met the third group of his "neighbors." Prior to this time he was not well known in the county, his acquaintance with neighbors having been limited to the River Families and some of the residents of Hyde Park. The places he frequented—St. James Church, the Hudson River Ice Yacht Club, the Harvard Club, ocean liners going to Europe—were not likely places to meet the average Dutchess County citizens that he would later learn to call "neighbor."

In FDR's memory the meeting with the political leaders of Dutchess County was a spontaneous event. Others remember it differently. James McGregor Burns suggested that John E. Mack visit FDR on a legal errand and propose he run for office. Karl Schriftgiesser, an earlier biographer, suggested that the idea of FDR running for the state senate seat was the brainchild of John K. Sague, the Mayor of Poughkeepsie. John Lindley reported that FDR went to meet the political leaders bareheaded and dressed in boots and riding breeches. Edward Perkins, Tammany Hall's man in Dutchess County, told FDR he would "have to take off those yellow shoes and put on some regular pants."[33]

By late October 1910, FDR had begun his political career and rode forth to meet his Dutchess County neighbors. Each morning at approximately 8:00 a.m. a bright red Maxwell touring car turned from the gates of Springwood onto the Post Road, not to return there until late in the day.[34] For twenty-eight days, FDR and his companions toured the 26th district in a manner both innovative and eye-catching. In Millerton, Wassaic, Dover Plains, Wingdale, Pawling, Gay Head, Wiccopee, Beekmanville, Green Haven, Stormville, Fishkill, Wapppingers, New Hamburg, Hughsonville, Chelsea and Matteawan, the message was the same:

> … my heart has grown glad and I have thanked God that it fell to my lot to be born and to have lived as one of the people of this Hudson Valley….with every new face that I have met it has been impressed upon me that we have a people that is truly American in the best sense of the word; a people alive, a people desirous of progress….[35]

For the first few years, much of FDR's power in Dutchess County lay in the area of patronage—the distribution of governmental jobs to the deserving and to the not so deserving. At this period of time the post office department controlled most of the federal spoils in a county like Dutchess. And in Washington, Roosevelt found himself close to the source of those jobs—the office of Albert S. Burleson, the Postmaster General.

Later, acting on advice from various county residents, FDR would involve himself more closely in county politics. In an early political activity after his illness, he was instrumental in having Philip A. Mylod elected to the post as Democratic County Chairman in 1923. As the Democratic vote in the county decreased instead of increasing, FDR sought to charm the members of the county committee. His political mentor and guide, Louis Howe, was more direct. At one point he offered FDR a more direct solution:

> My own remedy for the lackadaisical attitude of your own county committee would be to invite them to a picnic… offering them food or free anything…drop them into the creek with a weight around their necks….This would do a

world of good for the Democratic party in your county—
think it over.[36]

FDR's remedy was not so drastic—he would only replace
the county chairman, not drown the committeemen. So James
Townsend, former sheriff and postmaster and political crony,
succeeded Mylod as county chairman. By 1940, however, FDR
was once again looking to gain the political blessing of his county
neighbors. The selection of James Benson of Dover, was just the
latest revival of FDR's long-standing dream that someday the
Democrats could penetrate the Republican strongholds in the
outlying towns of the county. Throughout his political career in
the county his main approach to winning at the polls was through
patronage, public works in Democratic areas, personal, and political
favors. None seemed to bring the desired results, but Roosevelt
continued to call the citizens of the county "neighbor."

The flood of requests for favors on behalf of his Dutchess
County neighbors was unending. From the hamlet of Amenia came
a request for a donation to an Amenia Church where the winner of
a fund raising drive would receive a gold watch. FDR sent $5.00.[37]
The Methodist Church in Poughquag requested something for its
church fair. FDR sent $3.00.[38] From the executive director of the
Jewish Community Center in Poughkeepsie came a reminder that "a
statement from you on this occasion as a good neighbor would have
considerable influence on this drive for annual membership.". His
answer was calculated to give his neighbors a boost: "An unselfish
spirit which subordinates everything else to the common welfare is
the greatest asset a community can have."[39] Not all requests were
for money. At the requests of a group of Red Hook citizens, FDR
wrote to the state parole board for a pardon for a citizen of Red
Hook, noting that "neighbors in Red Hook were requesting the
pardon through him."[40] One local clergyman even wrote to request
a letter of introduction to the Pope, but FDR answered that it
would be contrary to established practice for a President to address
ecclesiastical dignitaries abroad."[41]

Often FDR's help would be sought because of the average citizen's inability to deal with the bureaucracies of the New Deal Government. A series of letters related to Alfred E. Bahret illustrates this problem. In the midst of the Depression, Bahret, the owner of a small florist business, sought relief for his mortgage indebtedness. The request was referred to the Farm Credit Administration, which then advised contacting the Home Owners Loan Corporation. They in turn felt the Farm Loan Association was the best source of help. Finally in January 1935 F.D.R. wrote to the Farm Credit Administration indicating that "this man (Mr. Bahret) is a neighbor of mine in Dutchess County."[42] The label of "neighbor" brought forth the desired results, a first mortgage loan of $6,700 for Mr. Roosevelt's "neighbor" in Dutchess County. Other county industry names appear in the President's Personal Files relating to war production and local affairs—Sedgwick Machine Works, Lumb Woodworking Company, International Business Machines, the Dutchess County Board of Supervisors.

In 1923 Henry MacCracken, President of Vassar College, would write to FDR noting that Vassar was "in great need of trustees who are neighbors of the college."[43] In his last campaign for the Presidency, C. Mildred Thompson, Dean of the College, would describe FDR as a "lover of trees" (land) and a "lover of people."[44]

Throughout his career FDR's "love of people" expressed itself in the manner in which he was interested in his neighbors and their county. This lover of land and people would spend the Presidential days searching for pragmatic solutions to the host of problems that were so adversely affecting the welfare of those people (economic depression, global conflict, and a myriad of local problems.) Perhaps the most incomprehensible fact about this complex man was that he, while perceiving of almost everyone as a "neighbor," remained a man alone. In the words of Sidney Shalett: "...the man who was rarely physically alone, became a man alone, a man lonely."[45]

In the fall of 1944 his loneliness caused him to write the national chairman that "all that is within me cries to go back to my home on the Hudson River." There, it was still possible in the world of his neighbors—the aristocrats of the River Families, the townspeople of Hyde Park, and the residents of his beloved Dutchess County—to find a way of life that was a source of strength and satisfaction. Strength and satisfaction were to be found there, even if never reflected in the political votes of those same neighbors and friends.

NOTES

1 Olin Dows, *Franklin Roosevelt at Hyde Park* (New York, New York: American Artists Group, 1949), p. 150.

2 Richard Hofstadter, *The American Political Tradition* (New York, New York: Alfred A. Knopf, Inc., 1949), p. 316.

3 James McGregor Burns, *Roosevelt: The Lion and the Fox* (New York, New York: Harcourt, Brace and Company, 1956), p.33.

4 FDR to F.F. Moon, 22 October 1915, Assistant Secretary of Navy Papers, Box 97, Franklin D. Roosevelt Library.

5 Olin Dows, *Franklin Roosevelt at Hyde Park*, p. 86

6 Poughkeepsie (New York) *Eagle-News*, 11, November 1940, p. 1

7 Franklin D. Roosevelt, President's Personal Files, #1589, Franklin D. Roosevelt Library.

8 William D. Hassett, *Off the Record With FDR 1942-1945* (New Brunswick, New Jersey: Rutgers University Press, 1958), p. 293.

9 Donald Scott Carmichael, *F.D.R.: Columnist* (Chicago, Illinois: Pelligriani and Cudahy, 1947), p.100.

10 Quoted in Richard Crowley, "Clermont and Rhinebeck's Sixteen Miles," *The Conservationist*, (May/June), pp. 23-24.

11 Sara Delano Roosevelt, Diary, Papers of Sarah D. Roosevelt, Roosevelt Family Papers, Box 67, FDRL.

12 *Poughkeepsie Sunday Courier*, 19 January 1913, p. 11.

13 Ibid. 7 January 1900, 19 January 1913, 25 June, 1916.

14 Martha Collins Bayne. *The Dutchess County Farmer* (Poughkeepsie, New York: Vassar College Norrie Fellowship Report, 1936), p. 72

15 FDR to Elizabeth Lynch, 23 December 1937, The President's Personal File, #5638, FDRL.

16 James McGregor Burns, "F.D.R., The Last Journey," *American Heritage*, Vol. XXI, No. 5 (August 1970), p. 78.

17 *Poughkeepsie* (New York) *Eagle News*, 10 October 1932.

18 Ibid.

19 William Hassett, *Off the Record with FDR 1942-1945*, pp. 64, 73, 102, 238, 246, 257.

20 Edmund P. Rogers to FDR, 4 October 1929, Roosevelt Family, Business, and Personal Papers, #72, FDRL.

21 Edmund P. Rogers to FDR, 8 October 1931, Roosevelt Family, Business, and Personal Papers, #72, FDRL. It is hard to imagine that St. James in the midst of the depression could need someone knowledgeable in "banking affairs" to keep their books.

22 Olin Dows, *Franklin D. Roosevelt at Hyde Park*, p. 147.

23 FDR to E. D. Meuser, 13 February 1913, Roosevelt New York State Senate Papers, Box 28, FDRL.

24 Maude Smith Rundall, Manuscript, 25 April 1938, President's Personal File, #1853, FDRL. Folder #8967, in the President's Personal Files, contains papers concerning the Hyde Park School System. and the various controversies involved.

25 Reeve Palmer to President Roosevelt (telegram to Warm Springs, Georgia), 26 January, 1938, President's Personal File, #1853, FDRL.

26 President's Personal File, #1853, FDRL.

27 Moses Smith to FDR, 28 November 1939, President's Personal File, #1930, FDRL.

28 FDR, "Remarks to Roosevelt Home Club," 31 August 1940, President's Personal File, #1820, FDRL.

29 FDR to Louis A. Simon [General Services Administration], 21 December 1939, President's Personal File, #1853, FDRL.

30 FDR to Edward Bruce, 22 October 1940, Olin Dows Papers, FDRL.

31 Robert Sherwood, *Roosevelt and Hopkins* (New York, New York: Harper and Brothers, 1968), p. 606.

32 Harold F. Gosnell, *Champion Campaigner* (New York, New York: Macmillan Company, 1952), p. 28.

33 Ernest K. Lindley, *Franklin Roosevelt: A Career in Progressive Democracy* (Indianapolis, Indiana: Bobbs Merrill Company, 1931), p. 28.

34 "'Hawkey' Trip with Roosevelt, *Poughkeepsie* (New York) *Evening Review*, 18 March 1935, copy of article found in Mylod Papers, FDRL. The quotation concerning Hawkey's occupation is taken from his letterhead on a letter to FDR, 10 October 1913, Assistant Secretary of Navy Papers, Box 146, FDRL.

35 *Hudson* (New York) *Valley Register*, 28 October 1910.

36 Louis M. Howe to FDR, 24 October 1928, Howe Papers, FDRL.

37 F. M. Burke to FDR, 28 August 1911, Roosevelt Family, Business and Personal Papers, #35, FDRL.

38 Poughquag Methodist Church to FDR, 8 July 1936, President's Personal File, #3903, FDRL.

39 Eli Kogos to FDR, 8 September 1939 and FDR to Eli Kogos, 9 September 1939, President's Personal File, #5511, FDRL.

40 FDR to M. Owen Potter, 6 January 1925, Family Business and Personal Papers, #35, FDRL.

41 FDR to Rev. Alexander Griswold, 21 June 1935, President's Personal File, #176, FDRL.

42 FDR to Governor Myer, 14 January 1935, President Personal File, #1853, FDRL

43 Henry MacCracken to FDR, 21 February 1923, President's Secretary's File, #145, FDRL.

44 C. Mildred Thompson, "F.D.R.—a Recollection and Appraisal," Unpublished manuscript, p. 6, Thompson Papers, FDRL.

45 Sidney Shalett, "Introduction," p. viii, in James Roosevelt, *Affectionately F.D.R.* (New York, New York: Harcourt, Brace and Company, 1959).

A Model for Local Historians?

Joyce C. Ghee

On April 3, 1931, Alexander C. Flick, the State Historian, received the following message from one of his most respected town historians:

> I wish that you would replace me as the local historian for the town of Hyde Park by appointing Mr. Benjamin Haviland in my place. I have literally no time to spend on the local history just now as you can well imagine and nothing has been done by me last year. Mr. Haviland is thoroughly qualified and knows the history better than anyone else.

This apologetic letter came on the Governor's stationery, signed by Franklin D. Roosevelt, who, in addition to holding the highest office in the state, had continued to serve as government historian for his hometown. This unusual state of affairs, while raising an ethical question or two, adds perspective to a unique career in government service.

Roosevelt, a Democrat, had been appointed by Republican Edward S. Foster, Hyde Park Supervisor, in June of 1926. Party politics, occasionally a factor in such decisions, seems to have had little bearing on the choice. Foster, pressed to action by the State Historian, declared in a letter, "Friend Franklin…as I know of

This article was originally written for the June 1991 issue of "History Directions," a publication of the New York State Museum. In the republishing process, it has been altered and re-edited to include additional related material. At the time of original writing, Ms. Ghee was Dutchess County Historian.

no one more competent I hope you will not object if I forward your name." Roosevelt had no objections, and it appears from correspondence among his personal papers in the Franklin D. Roosevelt Library that both he and Flick were pleased with the Supervisor's choice.

Foster's appointee brought prestige, knowledge and experience to the position. A lawyer and family man with Hudson Valley roots, Roosevelt had already served as a New York State Senator, held a post in Washington as Assistant Secretary of the Navy, and had been considered as a candidate for national office. He was dealing courageously with the changes in his life after his polio attack in 1921 by renewing state and national political ties, writing, speaking, and involving himself in public issues. He had also, on several past occasions, evidenced his interest in town history and a willingness to be of service to its leaders. He proved to be an effective and productive historian, who, according to John Ferris, former Archivist at the FDR Library, "saw history as a tool to serve his ever expanding community …"

His view of his official role and the power of local history as a community resource tool were ahead of his time, akin to public or social history. It was born, not of academic leanings, but of a strong personality, confident of the importance of his family and social position and nourished by access to information and power. The result, evolving since his youth, was a philosophy of public office rooted in a knowledge of history, securely in the hands of a political pragmatist and activist.

Those who subscribe to the theory that local historians are born and not made may well see familiar patterns reflected in FDR's rites of passage into their midst: absorption in family and community history, involvement in civic matters, respect for tradition. FDR gleaned both knowledge and access from associations developed through the Holland Society (1910) and as a charter member of the Dutchess County Historical Society (1914). His immersion in genealogy and adventures with local architecture has been well documented by biographers and academics.

He was also a shrewd and instinctive collector, willing to bargain or wait out the professional auctioneers for items that took his eye. His forays into the libraries and holdings of the River Families expressed educated acquisitiveness driven by concern for the protection of fragile community, cultural and documentary resources. Roosevelt's gatherings brought us the first presidential library in this nation's history. Conceived long before it was opened in 1939, the FDR Library grew around an extensive personal local history collection, intended to be under the care of a friend and colleague, Dutchess County Historian Helen Wilkinson Reynolds.

FDR was deeply concerned with preservation and accessibility of local history and traditions, and convinced of the correctness of his own vision. He operated independently, using or ignoring political and bureaucratic processes as they suited his purposes. Self-confidence guided his actions before, during and after his tenure as Hyde Park Town Historian. He applied energetically whatever resources were available to the tasks at hand: people, funds, offices, information. Although he was a capable researcher, powerful writer and speaker, and conversant with library and museum protocols, he preferred to gather into the fold partners whose exceptional talent in specific areas would enhance a project. Be it a book, research project, survey, creation of a public building modeled on a local landmark, or plan for mural design, he encouraged and accepted only the best and most historically accurate. He usually chose for himself the roles of executive producer or editor, which allowed him to influence the final product and oversee the smallest details and to use his considerable political and didactic skills to the fullest.

Town board minutes, even before his appointment as Town Historian, provide small insights to his methods:

April 1, 1920
Motion: Be it resolved that the Town board of the Town of Hyde Park accepted the German machine gun from the Navy Department to be used for exhibit purposes, and be it further resolved that the clerk be directed to thank the Hon.

F.D. Roosevelt, Asst. Secry [sic] of the Navy for his efforts in furnishing the same.

The gun is still in place on the Town Hall lawn.

> December 16, 1922
> Motion: that the following resolution be accepted and a copy sent to the Towns of Clinton and Pleasant Valley: Whereas the Hon. Franklin D. Roosevelt being desirous of having published a history of the town of Hyde Park and that the cost thereof be met by public subscription; therefore be it resolved that this board authorizes the publication of such history and that the towns of Clinton and Pleasant Valley be asked to appoint a committee to cooperate with Mr. Roosevelt in this work.

The book, conceived before his appointment, was done with private monies, published by the Dutchess County Historical Society in 1928 as *Records of the Town of Hyde Park in Dutchess County.*

The absence of any reference to the town historian in minutes during his tenure (1926-1933) is also telling. There is no mention of his appointment or resignation therein. Indications are that he dealt directly thereafter with the State Historian. He took no salary, viewing the position as a civic duty for a man of social standing, and he found the wherewithal for projects of his own design among friends, colleagues, and allies. He also retained, eventually to be deposited in the presidential library, correspondence, annual reports, research, and records relating to his activities while town historian. Although he may be faulted for this as an appointed official, it is apparent that he felt that he was more to be entrusted with valuable archival records than were those who for a short time might occupy elective office in town.

That Roosevelt was an imperial local historian can scarcely be doubted. He was a product of his era and social caste. There is no arguing either with his legacy—to the local community, the state, the nation, and the world. The list of his historical bequests is almost endless. It includes materials as esoteric as documents such as "Proceedings of the Stoutsburg Religious Society 1789" (found among the thousands of papers and materials in the FDR Library) and extends to a vision of local vernacular architecture as an historical tool shaping a sense of place in communities all across America. It encompasses public policies that encourage research, preservation, and the education of future generations. Hyde Park retains, among such items on this short list: the German gun, the first presidential library in the nation's history, two national historic sites, a town library, post office and three schools modeled on local landmarks built of stone in the local Dutch tradition. There also was undertaken an enormously valuable body of local historical research. Town and community institutional records were collected, transcribed, published and archived by and because of this man. He influenced others to follow suit and, like a great wave, his vision engulfed a generation, bringing them back to review their values and goals in the spotlight of history.

While our generation of government historians cannot (nor may they wish to) imitate his every strategy, there is much to be learned in revisiting the accomplishments of this memorable local historian.

ACKNOWLEDGMENTS

I am indebted to those who initially assisted with information and advice. They include: Diane Boyce, former Hyde Park Historian; Ethel Whitney, former Hyde Park Deputy Town Clerk; Eileen Hayden, Director of the Dutchess County Historical Society; and John Ferris, former Archivist with the FDR Library. I am grateful to Alicia Vivona, Archivist, FDR Library, for her assistance in locating materials helpful in revising the article.

BIBLIOGRAPHY

Family and Personal Papers, boxes 25, 26, 41. Franklin D. Roosevelt Collections, FDR Library, Hyde Park, N.Y.

Ferris, John C. "Franklin D. Roosevelt: His Development and Accomplishments as a Local Historian." *Dutchess County Historical Society Year Book*, Vol. 68 (1983): 16-39. Dutchess County Historical Society, Poughkeepsie, N.Y.

Hyde Park Town Records: November 15, 1914 to December 28, 1935. Hyde Park Town Hall, Hyde Park, N.Y.

Rhoads, William B. "Helen Wilkinson Reynolds, FDR and Hudson Valley Architecture." *Dutchess County Historical Society Year Book*, Vol. 68 (1983): 4-15. Dutchess County Historical Society, Poughkeepsie, N.Y.

The Beacon-Fishkill Connection

Willa Skinner

In October 1910, Morgan Hoyt, Town of Fishkill Democratic Chairman, and Major James Forrestal were on their way to Poughkeepsie as delegates to the Democratic State Convention to hear a "young chap from up Hyde Park way" receive the nomination for State Senator. The name was Roosevelt, and as a candidate he had made a favorable impression on the two committeemen at a previous meeting in Albany. Hoyt later described him as being "of perfect physique, with ruddy cheeks and that invariable smile which was to be such a big asset to him later in life. With that look of determination and assurance which won for him so many bitter political battles, he promised he would put all the energy he possessed into a winning fight."[1]

James Forrestal was a Matteawan businessman who had built a successful construction company and was active in political circles. The title of Major was bestowed through his service in the New York National Guard. Morgan Hoyt was editor and publisher of the *Matteawan Journal*, the leading Democratic newspaper in southern Dutchess County, which covered the twin villages of Matteawan and Fishkill Landing. Not only did Roosevelt have his start here, but it also was the beginning of a life-long friendship

Willa Skinner is the Town of Fishkill Historian. For forty years she wrote and edited a weekly general interest column for the Southern Dutchess News *and* Beacon Free Press. *She has written a history of Fishkill and Southern Dutchess, "Signal Fires in the Highlands," and has taught a class at Dutchess Community College: Researching Your House Roots. She is presently conducting research on the Revolutionary War Supply Depot at Fishkill.*

FDR campaigning at Bank Square, Beacon, November 1936. BEACON HISTORICAL SOCIETY.

between the newspaper publisher and the future president.[2]

With less than four weeks to go before Election Day, a small crowd gathered at Bank Square in Fishkill Landing to hear Franklin Roosevelt deliver the first campaign speech of his career. Morgan Hoyt, called Morg by friends and colleagues, introduced him, thereby setting a precedent, for Roosevelt would return to the same spot for every election campaign, and would always insist that Morg introduce him.

Morg Hoyt would introduce him once again as a senator, twice as a candidate for governor, and four times for the presidency in the exact spot where he made his first campaign speech. On the day before the election in 1944, when he was running for an unprecedented fourth term as president, Roosevelt told the assembled crowd in Bank Square, "Morgan Hoyt has been introducing me for 100 years"[3] Years later Hoyt wrote in his newspaper column, "It is doubtful if any of Roosevelt's speeches of later years seemed more important to him that did that first speech."[4]

In the audience that day was eighteen-year-old James Forrestal, Jr., youngest son of the Major, a talented and ambitious cub reporter on the *Matteawan Journal* who was being groomed by Hoyt for a career in journalism but instead left the confines of his home town to attend Princeton and make a career on Wall Street. Would anyone have dreamed then that Jim Forrestal, whose roots went back to the old village of Matteawan, would one day be appointed by President Franklin D. Roosevelt, first as Assistant Secretary of the Navy, then Secretary of the Navy during World War II, and would subsequently serve as the nation's first Secretary of Defense under Truman?

Roosevelt was a guest at the Forrestal house in Matteawan during the senate campaign,[5] and no doubt the Major's son must have heard and absorbed much of the political talk. The Forrestal house still stands as a landmark on Fishkill Avenue in what is now Beacon, looking much the same structurally as it did in 1910. It is privately owned. A plaque in front notes that it was the boyhood home of James Forrestal, first U.S. Secretary of Defense.

The Republican newspaper, The *Fishkill Standard*, virtually ignored the Roosevelt campaign, believing that the Democratic candidate would not win, as a Democrat had not won the district since 1856. But Hoyt's *Matteawan Journal* displayed Roosevelt's picture prominently. The Democratic committee took an ad headed, "Pledged to Serve the People! Vote for Him for State Senator!" It was followed by the text of John Mack's nominating speech, which included a notation addressed to the farming community, an important segment of the voting population in Dutchess, Putnam, and Columbia counties, which comprised the constituency of the district. "He has lived all his life in a farming community and is in quick sympathy with this large class of population," the ad stated.[6]

An important matter was brought up at the first committee meeting. Election Day was less than a month away. Should they forget about a horse and buggy and use an automobile to get out into the country where they could meet more people, especially farmers in isolated areas? Hoyt pointed out that farmers mistrusted the newfangled horseless carriages. Horses didn't like them and when meeting one on the road would bolt, turn around, and sometimes upset a farmer's loaded wagon.

The decision: Go with the automobile. They would hire the only machine available between New York and Albany—a red Maxwell touring car, rented for $20 a day, with no windshield and no top. Bedecked with flags, the car set off from Bank Square while a crowd gathered to see the novelty.

In one day the Maxwell covered Millerton, Amenia, Dover and Wassaic in the afternoon, and in the evening a big meeting in Pawling. The car occasionally had to stop to keep from frightening farmers' horses. Roosevelt made speeches in farm barnyards, apple orchards, and even from the tops of haystacks, living up to the promise of a whirlwind campaign. At one time the Maxwell overshot the New York border and the young senate hopeful found himself haranguing crowds in Connecticut that couldn't vote for him anyway.[7] The decision to rent the Maxwell paid off. No candidate had reached so many people before. Roosevelt won by a close majority of 1,140.

In the state Senate he was named chairman of the Forest, Fish and Game Committee and he appointed Morgan Hoyt as committee clerk. Hoyt's job, however, was short-lived. It did not even last a day. But let Morg tell the story in his own words:

> "He gave me the job and took me into "Packey" McCabe's office. McCabe was Albany's Democratic leader and was in the Senate. McCabe gave me the necessary stationery in the office and, calling a page, told him to escort me, which he did. As I put away the stationery and sat down in the swivel chair and gazed out of the window at Albany, I thought Roosevelt was quite a guy to be able to give a chap a job like mine.
>
> "The next morning I was surprised to see the door ajar. I had the key and wondered why Roosevelt was up so early. As I went in, there sat a big red man wearing a derby. I said,

'Good Morning.' He reeled in his chair and in an angry tone bellowed. 'Who are you?' In a meek voice I replied, 'I'm clerk of this committee.' He rose and cried out, 'You are like hell. I'm clerk of this committee.' As I looked at his height and countenance I said to myself, 'You are right. I'm not going to dispute you.' "

Roosevelt sought out party leader McCabe, who was very apologetic, but the big man in the derby had been given the job by the Tammany machine years before, and it was difficult to unseat him. "So Roosevelt's first political appointee," said Hoyt, "held his job only a few hours." [8]

At this time the villages of Matteawan and Fishkill Landing were planning to merge and form a new city in southern Dutchess County, but disputes continued over the choice of a name. Major Forrestal kept Senator Roosevelt informed of the situation. The people of Matteawan, he said, did not want to give up their historic name. At first they disapproved of the name Beacon but the name won out, and on March 15, 1913 a charter was granted to the new city of Beacon, named for the Revolutionary War signal fires that lay in readiness on the summit of Mount Beacon to warn of the approach of enemy ships on the Hudson.

Hoyt established a new newspaper, the *Beacon Journal*, with Ed Hayden as editor. In later years, after Roosevelt became president, Hayden was fond of telling people he used to be Roosevelt's boss —and he was, for a time. In 1921, when Roosevelt was recuperating from polio in Hyde Park, Hayden proposed that FDR write a weekly column for the Journal. He accepted the assignment and for several months was a regular contributor. Hayden considered himself fortunate, not only in getting a writer whose commentaries were widely quoted in other newspapers, but he took no pay for the job.[9]

Ed Hayden worked on newspapers in Beacon, Newburgh and Poughkeepsie for thirty years. He ended his career as political reporter for the *Newburgh News* three years before his death in 1958 at the age of 60. He was a member of the press corps that covered the President's funeral services in Hyde Park, and his obituary in *The New York Times* on April 11, 1958 noted that he at one time had FDR on his staff as a regular columnist.

Morgan Hoyt remained a friend of FDR through the years. On his retirement from publishing, he wrote a column entitled, "Turning Back the Clock," for the *Beacon Evening News* from the 1940s until his death in 1953 at the age of 89.

NOTES

1 Hoyt, Morgan, "Turning Back the Clock," a series of columns appearing in the *Beacon Evening News*, 1946-1953. Collections of the Beacon Historical Society.

2 MacCracken, Henry N. *Blithe Dutchess*, (1958) p. 85.

3 Hoyt, "Turning Back" (undated).

 Hoopes, Townsend and Brinckley, Douglas, *Driven Patriot—The Life and Times of James Forestall* (1992), p. 11.

4 Hoyt, "Turning Back."

5 Hoopes & Brinckley, p. 11.

6 *Matteawan Journal*, October 8, 1910.

7 Gunther, John, *Roosevelt in Retrospect* (1950), p. 203. Miller, Nathan, *FDR—An Intimate History* (1983) p. 85. There are different versions of the Maxwell story. Miller said it was a gaudy vehicle. Hoyt said it was bright red, two-seated and high in front. Roosevelt later recalled it as a dusty old red Maxwell. Hoyt said it was the only car for rent between here and Albany.

8 Hoyt, "Turning Back."

9 Hayden obituaries, *New York Herald Tribune* and *New York Times*, April 10, 1958. Conversations with Hayden's nephew, journalist Dick Shea of Beacon (died 2001).

The 1910 Senate Campaign

Joan Spence

FDR never won an election in Dutchess County—fact or fiction?

When I lost the November 1993 election to become a county legislator representing part of Hyde Park, many people tried to console me saying: "We're not surprised. Democrats cannot win in Dutchess County. Even FDR never carried Hyde Park or the county."

In fact, FDR did win in Hyde Park and Dutchess County, not always, but at least sometimes. And other Democrats have won, too. The first time FDR ran for State Senator in 1910 he carried his hometown and his county and again in his 1912 race for re-election. He also won in the 1914 Democratic primary for U.S. Senator, and in his 1930 bid to be re-elected New York State Governor.

An intriguing aside: What if FDR had lost the 1910 election? Would he have remained a Wall Street lawyer, Eleanor Roosevelt a shy member of the Junior League? However influential a figure FDR later proved to be on the state, national and international scenes, like every other political figure he had to begin his political career with a local base.

Why did he win in 1910, especially in Hyde Park and Dutchess County, traditionally Republican strongholds, then as now? For example, a comparison of the 1910 voter registration figures of the

Joan Spence is a graduate of Smith College. She served as an assistant to Dutchess County Executive Lucille Pattison from 1980 to 1991. Together with Joyce Ghee, Spence formed a consulting business and co-authored four books. As she relates in this article, reprinted from Dutchess Magazine *(Fall 1994), she ran for the county legislature in 1993 as a Democrat representing part of Hyde Park.*

second and third election districts in Hyde Park with those of the 34th legislative district in 1993 shows:

Total	Democrats	Republicans	Non-enrolled	Other
1910 : 513	187 36%	255 50%	58 11%	13 2%
1993 : 2950	784 27%	1063 36%	999 34%	104 3%

Hyde Park has grown significantly, and the percentages of Democrats and of Republicans have decreased while the percentage of non-enrolled voters has notably increased. Nevertheless, Republicans still predominate.

Since FDR won the Hyde Park districts 293 to 154, he had to attract Republican voters. Obviously his name and family connections, his effective and technologically modern campaign, his personality were all contributing factors. However, his victory was as much a continuation of a trend of Republican losses as a personal success. Sixty-eight years later, the election of a Democrat, Lucille P. Pattison, as Dutchess County Executive, was also attributable in part to Republican disarray. The Republican County Executive had pleaded guilty to bribery.

Republican scandals and the 1906 election

Key then to an understanding of FDR's victory in 1910 is an awareness of the political events of the previous few years, which had severely weakened the appeal of the Republican Party. Prior to 1906, Dutchess County had returned Republican pluralities ranging from 3,000 to 5,000, and very few Democrats had served the district in the State Senate since 1856. However, the Democrat Party was gaining strength. Lewis Stuyvesant Chanler and Robert Winthrop Chanler, J.W. and Silas Hinkley, Frank Hasbrouck, John Mylod, John Mack, Edward Perkins were among the prominent county Democrats.

The unprecedented Democratic victories in 1906 hinged on the so-called Hicks case. Willet Hicks, a "taxpayer," brought a citizen's

SPEAKING TOUR

Hon. Richard E. Connell

Democratic candidate for Member of Congress

Franklin D. Roosevelt ‖ **Ferdinand A. Hoyt**

*Candidate for
State Senator, and* ‖ *Candidate for
Member of Assembly*

Desiring to meet the voters and discuss with
them the issues of the campaign will speak at,
the following meetings:

Monday, October 24th, 1910.

Millerton, R. R. Station	12 o'clock
Amenia, Bank Square	1 P. M.
Wassaic, R. R. Station	2 P. M.
Dover Plains, R. R. Station	3 P. M.
South Dover, Trowbridge's Store	4 P. M.
Wingdale, R. R. Station	5 P. M.
And Big Evening Rally at Pawling, St. John's Lyceum	7:30 P. M.

Tuesday, October 25th, 1910.

Patterson, R. R. Station	10:30 A. M.
Holmes, R. R. Station	11:30 A. M.
West Pawling, R. R. Station	12:30 P. M.
Poquag, Frank Brill's Store	1:30 P. M.
Beekman, Front of Store	2:30 P. M.
Green Haven, on Square	3:30 P. M.
Stormville, R. R. Station	4:30 P. M.
And Large Evening Meeting at Hopewell Junction, in the Hall	8 P. M.

Wednesday, October 26th, 1910.

Gay Head	10 A. M.
Wicopee	11 A. M.
Fishkill Village, front Van Wyck Hall	12 o'clock
Wappingers Falls, Village Square	1:30 P. M.
New Hamburgh, R. R. Station	3 P. M.
Hughsonville, 4 Corners	4 P. M.
And Open Air Mass Meetings at Fishkill Landing, Bank Square	7 P. M.
Matteawan, Fountain Square	8:30 P. M.

FDR schedule, 1910 Senate campaign. FDR PRESIDENTIAL LIBRARY.

action against the Board of Supervisors and former Sheriff Allan H.
Hoffman to show that the Sheriff's 1902-1903 bills of $22,000 to
cover the costs of boarders at the jail, reimbursement for mileage for
serving summons, and other work were fraudulent and illegal. At
that time the Sheriff was unsalaried and charged the county for his

services. In the summer of 1906 the case was heard before a referee.

Headlines from *The News-Press*, "the oldest Democratic daily in the state" published by Silas and J.W. Hinkley, give the flavor of the case: "Many in Bill Not in Jail Shown in Sheriff's Case—Boys Whose Names Are Spread Upon the Criminal Records of Dutchess County Swear That They Were Never in Jail at All—Mileage Charges Which Seem to Show No Travel" and "…Nine Payrolls in the Court House—Janitor Paid for Court House Work When There Was No Court House" and "…Police Officers Remember Very Few Things."

The Eagle, a Republican newspaper, was more restrained in its coverage, pointing out the discrepancies in the bills were minor and that the hearings were themselves very "tedious" as indeed they must have been with the introduction of more than 1,092 exhibits!

It was within the context of the publicity about this case that the Republicans and Democrats held their conventions to nominate candidates for the 1906 elections. At their convention the Republicans clashed over candidates for Sheriff. The Republican Committee Chairman warned the convention "there is strong sentiment in the county against the Sheriff's bills," and "I don't say the sentiments are just, but I believe the nomination of a man who might be referred to as a friend of Mr. Hoffman [the Sheriff] will work harm to the party." However, the convention ignored this advice and nominated H. Freemont Vandewater, who, as a Supervisor representing the Town of Hyde Park, had approved the Sheriff's bills.

The Democrats nominated Robert Winthrop Chanler, brother of Lewis Stuyvesant Chanler, one of the lawyers for Mr. Hicks, and himself the Democratic candidate for Lieutenant Governor.

The two candidates presented quite a contrast. Mr. Vandewater, a self-made man, was a butcher. According to *The Eagle*, "His political growth has not been of a mushroom character, nurtured into quick existence by the lavish expenditure of inherited wealth…" Robert Chanler, on the other hand, had been educated at the Beaux Arts School of Architecture in Paris and later went to Rome "where he studied for future perfection." A person of independent means who decorated mansions in New York with his works of art, he was also touted as being an expert farmer.

Robert Chanler zeroed in on his ability to run the Sheriff's office on $10,000 a year, half of what the incumbent seemed to have spent. He advertised widely, and tied his opponent to the Sheriff's bills. According to his grandson, Bronson Chanler, he also gave elaborate picnics, sponsored marching bands, and rode around the county with Richard Harding Davis, wearing Western chaps, a ten-gallon hat, and a six shooter! The Chanlers built up quite a Democratic organization.

The Democrats swept the county. Robert Chanler was elected Sheriff and John E. Mack, District Attorney. Mr. Chanler carried the county by 2,248, but lost Hyde Park, his opponent's hometown. Mr. Mack carried Dutchess County by 1,524 and Hyde Park 397 to 324. John Sague was elected Mayor of the City of Poughkeepsie, and Lewis Stuyvesant Chanler, Lieutenant Governor.

"Sheriff Bob" Chanler served one term as sheriff, not seeking re-election in 1909. Nevertheless, once again the Democrats won, electing their candidates for Sheriff, Assembly (Lewis Stuyvesant Chanler), County Clerk, Treasurer and District Attorney, with Mr. Mack leading the ticket with a plurality of 2,051. While 20 towns elected Democratic Supervisors, Hyde Park elected H. Freemont Vandewater, former Republican candidate for Sheriff and father of John B. Vandewater, who later became county attorney. John F. Schlosser, Mr. Mack's opponent in 1906, was elected State Senator and Hamilton Fish, a Republican, Congressman.

FDR, willing candidate in 1910

This then was the background for FDR's 1910 campaign. He was a young (only 28) and politically untried newcomer. Edward Perkins, Chairman of the Democratic Party, and John Mack, the District Attorney, first approached him to run for the Second Assembly District seat as they seemed to have thought that Lewis Chanler, the Democratic incumbent, was ready to retire. However, Mr. Chanler evidently saw no reason to step aside for FDR.

When it became obvious that FDR would have to run for the State Senate rather than for the Assembly, John Mack gave him only one chance in five of victory. FDR's opponent, John F. Schlosser was the incumbent, a well-known lawyer, reputedly eloquent, and the president of the State Firemen's Association.

The Roosevelt name

What accounts for FDR's victory? Certainly the name "Roosevelt" was well known throughout the United States. While it is sometimes thought Eleanor Roosevelt made the "good" marriage, it was in fact she who was the niece of Theodore Roosevelt, a Republican, former Governor of New York State and President of the United States.

FDR admired TR and listened to him when he reiterated time and time again the theme of the obligation of public service for men of good background and education. The *New York Herald* noted in an October news story: "The candidacy of Franklin D. Roosevelt, of Dutchess, a relative of Colonel Roosevelt, for State Senator, on the Democratic ticket, is worrying Republican leaders because of its widespread influence upon the party vote."

As important to FDR in his election efforts as his connection to TR, however, was his own family, especially the example of his father, a Democrat. James Roosevelt had served as Town Supervisor and as a trustee of the local schools. Grant Dickinson, a Democrat who had been barely defeated for Town Supervisor in 1909, recalled years afterwards that James Roosevelt took his position as school trustee seriously and used to actually visit the school. In 1910 The *Patterson News Weekly* noted that James Roosevelt was well known and "kindly remembered everywhere for his kindness of heart and for the good he was constantly doing." People spoke of the sincerity of FDR's father and his example of good citizenship. The family name and connections were not the only or most important explanation for his success. TR's own son failed in his political efforts. And much later, even the Rockefeller name and fortune failed to gain the presidency for Nelson Rockefeller.

A *"strenuous" campaign*

From the time of his official nomination on Oct. 6, FDR ran an excellent campaign. In his nominating speech John Mack noted the public was astonished by the disclosures of "graft and dishonesty of public officials,"—a reference to the Republicans. In his acceptance speech FDR said he was grateful for the "opportunity to do what little I can to advance the cause of good government under the banner of the Democratic Party this year." He stressed his "absolute independence" saying "I am pledged to no man; I am influenced by no specific interest, and so I shall remain," and said that he would run a "strenuous" campaign, and he did.

Hard work helps to account for FDR's victory. His attention to detail already manifested in his hobbies—stamp collecting and bird cataloging—stood him in good stead. He was very thorough.

Driving around the district in a red Maxwell

Upon his nomination FDR rented a red Maxwell automobile and during the four weeks before the election drove 2,000 miles around the district. He later recalled that they drove "at the dangerous pace of 22 miles an hour in Mr. [Harry T.] Hawkey's old red Maxwell, without any front windshields, without any top—an old Maxwell that when we met a horse or team—and that was about every half mile or so…we had to stop, not only stop, but stop the engine." Aside from the scheduled talks in front of post offices, at cross roads, town halls, FDR stopped to speak to all those he encountered. He also made sure that the schedules of stops were well publicized and even published in the newspapers.

Mr. Hawkey pointed out that FDR was never late to an appointment despite the supposed unreliability of automobiles; they had only one flat tire during the entire campaign. They covered between 50 and 150 miles a day, leaving Hyde Park about 8 a.m. and returning late in the evening. At the same time, FDR's opponent, Scholsser, was using a horse drawn carriage.

Indicative of the success of FDR's approach was an attack by Hamilton Fish, the Republican candidate for Congress, who called the trip "a vaudeville tour for the benefit of farmers." FDR countered by rhetorically asking whether Ham Fish had sneered because the car had American flags on it or "because we did a thing he never did. We went among the whole section, and gave the people a chance to see their candidates, to meet them face to face…?"

Hamilton Fish also suggested that FDR was not a resident of the district, having become a New York City lawyer. FDR replied: "I have lived in Hyde Park ever since I happened to be born there. I live in Hyde Park now, and I expect to die there."

Issues and independence

During the 1910 campaign, perhaps somewhat ingenuously, FDR noted the difficulty of focusing on particular issues and continued to emphasize his own independence. In a move, which was politically, astute and most probably principled, too, FDR acknowledged his support of Charles Evans Hughes, the Republican governor who had resigned that October to become an Associate Justice of the Supreme Court. Governor Hughes had recommended direct nominations for U.S. Senators as opposed to the practice of nominations by state party conventions, while John F. Schlosser, FDR's opponent, had aroused the ire of groups such as the Pomona Grange by voting against Governor Hughes' position. The Grange sent a letter to the newspaper, writing: "I know some good Republicans who think that the senator's action…was an indication that the will of the party machine at Albany was more important than the wishes of his constituents." FDR hammered away at the "rotten corruption of the New York State Legislature and the extravagant mismanagement of the state administration." And close to home, he inveighed against the "evil conditions" which had existed in the county and City of Poughkeepsie until they were thoroughly cleaned under the leadership of men such as Mayor John Sague and District Attorney John Mack. His reference to Mr. Mack was particularly apt as it was reported that the District Attorney had been successful in stopping an "epidemic of pilfering and chicken stealing," an issue of concern to the many farmers of the county.

Money—As important then as now

In all elections, issues are only as important as the means by which they are articulated and made known to the voters. Money counts. In fact, *The Eagle* had greeted the news of FDR's nomination: "They [the Democrats] have made a new and valuable discovery—Franklin D. Roosevelt, younger son of the late James Roosevelt of Hyde Park… Presumably his contribution to the campaign funds goes well above the five figures, hence the value of his discovery…" While this estimate proved high, the budget of FDR's campaign was almost $2,000.

FDR advertised widely in many district newspapers. At that time in the City of Poughkeepsie alone there were two daily morning and two daily afternoon papers as well as a semi-weekly. The record of campaign expenses which he carefully kept shows $717.56 spent on advertising. From Poughkeepsie, home of *The Enterprise* ($98), the News Co. ($57.45), and *The Eagle* ($127) to The *Patterson Weekly News* ($12) he made sure that his name and photograph were before the voters. One advertisement stressed his independence, his Hyde Park roots, the advantage of his trained mind as a lawyer, and his sympathy for the farmers. Another featured an endorsement by a prominent Republican lawyer, Henry H. Wells of Brewster.

Personality

Perhaps the single most important element in FDR's victory was his own personality. Tom Leonard, a Hyde Park Democratic Committeeman, recalled his first meeting with FDR. Mr. Leonard was painting FDR's brother's house when FDR appeared to ask him about obtaining the nomination. "Call me Franklin," said he.

Tom Leonard noted that FDR always asked people for their advice. He was a "top-notch salesman," approaching people as a neighbor or friend and then leading to the fact that he was a candidate for office. When meeting people, he conveyed the impression that he was taking a personal interest in their affairs.

FDR had a sense of humor. He received a letter dated Nov. 1 from the Republican State Committee asking him for a $50 donation as otherwise "Democratic success at this election will put under Democratic control the one hundred millions the state is spending for the Barge Canal, the fifty millions for good roads... It will enable the Democratic Party to re-district the Congressional Districts of this state so that for 10 years 25 Democratic Congressmen will probably be elected in place of 12 as at present... In his reply dated Nov. 9, the day after the election, FDR wrote: "I appreciate your courtesy in sending me the enclosed appeal. I have used it with great effect in my campaign..."

And finally, of course, there was sheer good luck. Nothing went wrong in his campaign and that of his opponent never captured the imagination of the voter.

The present and the future

More than 80 years later, descendants of some of the families prominent in Democratic politics in 1910 are now well known in other arenas. John E. Mack is chairman of Central Hudson, John Mylod is director of the Clearwater while his sister, Eileen Mylod Hayden, is the Executive Director of the Dutchess County Historical Society. Winthrop Aldrich, a grand nephew of the Chanlers, serves in the New York State Department of Parks and Recreation. And the Hinkleys have recently served the public interest as elected officials. David Hinkley, a Democrat, was the Supervisor of the Town of Poughkeepsie, 1989-1991, while his son Patrick, a Republican, was elected Councilman in the Fifth Ward of the town in 1993.*

When I ran, there was enormous cynicism on the part of the voters. They simply did not believe much that they heard, and I am sad to say that in general they are right. Where are the candidates who are willing to lead rather than to follow the shifting opinions of the public as reflected in polls? Where are those to whom involvement in the political sphere is a form of public service? Where are those willing to take a chance, running against the odds as FDR did in 1910, Lucille Pattison did in 1978, Eileen Hickey did in 1992? In 1993, 14 of 35 seats on the Dutchess County Legislature were uncontested.

As I found out, sometimes you lose. But sometimes, like FDR, former County Executive Lucille Pattison, and Assemblywoman Eileen Hickey, you win. Rather than ever again being consoled by the erroneous "fact" that FDR could not win in Hyde Park and Dutchess County, Democrats might take heart at his 1910 victory and strive to repeat it again and again. Who knows, another time, there may even be a red Maxwell for hire!

*Editor's Note: This article has been reprinted as originally published. Some of the individuals mentioned above may no longer hold the positions noted.

Franklin and Eleanor: Presidential Neighbors

Elizabeth A. Daniels

Franklin Roosevelt, Local Trustee:
A College/Community Commitment

My dear Dr. MacCracken,

Your letter of Feb 21st has finally found me down among the Florida Keys, and though I have had no official communication from the secretary of the Board of Trustees I am more than pleased with the action of the Board of Trustees at their last meeting. It is going to be a great pleasure for me to come into closer association with Vassar College and I am particularly looking forward, also, to seeing you more frequently and more intimately.

Naturally, also, I am hopeful that I will be able to help in bringing the college into closer association with Dutchess County. Until you came to Vassar, we who had lived in the neighborhood for many years knew very little about the college or its work. In fact, for most of us Vassar might just as well have been a thousand miles away.

—Franklin Roosevelt, February 1923[1]

Thus began an association between the Roosevelts and the college that lasted until the death of Eleanor Roosevelt in November 1962. While Franklin was a trustee for many years, active or honorary,

Elizabeth Daniels (Vassar Class of 1941) is Professor Emerita of English at Vassar College. Currently she is the college historian and is the author of several books. The following is the first half of a chapter from her book, Bridges to the World: Henry Noble MacCracken and Vassar College, *College Avenue Press, Clinton Corners, NY, 1994. Used with permission.*

from 1923 until his death, Eleanor was a friend and frequent visitor. In the first years of the association, Franklin had more to do with the college than Eleanor; after a while, and especially after he became President, it was the other way around. Many times when Eleanor was in Hyde Park she would send down her car to the campus to pick up some Vassar students to come for a visit, or she might drive down herself, popping up on the campus—the invited guest for a meal of the students in the cooperative house—or for a lecture, or to give a talk at the Vassar Summer Institute of Euthenics in the summertime.

As Roosevelt's gubernatorial and presidential jobs often caused him to be absent from Dutchess County, his visits to the college became less frequent, whereas Eleanor's kept up steadily over the years of her life. Occasionally the MacCrackens were invited to an event at the summer White House on the river at Hyde Park. During the World Youth Congress held at Vassar in the summer of 1938, Eleanor Roosevelt's presence at the conference, in which she was keenly interested, opened a new dimension in her relationship with Noble MacCracken. She came to his defense in the midst of many attacks from the right, which alleged that Vassar was making itself available to house the congress of an imputed communist group.

As America debated intervention on behalf of England and the Allies in 1940, however, MacCracken and Roosevelt approached a parting of the ways. MacCracken thought America's entry into the war would resolve nothing, and he was opposed to Churchill's position and the joint agreement of Roosevelt and Churchill adopted as the Atlantic Charter. On the Vassar campus, MacCracken had very few supporters among the faculty for his anti-involvement position, although among the students there were some who strongly agreed. As campus wartime tensions and anxieties increased in 1939, and until America's entrance into the war in December 1941, MacCracken's position, especially among his fellow administrators, became rather isolated with respect to the war issues. His colleague C. Mildred Thompson, the dean, was very

FDR and Henry Noble MacCracken, Vassar College Commencement, June 9, 1931.
VASSAR COLLEGE SPECIAL COLLECTIONS

much a supporter of Churchill's position, and their relationship became noticeably strained when, in the spring of 1940, Thompson promoted a petition among the faculty urging the president of the United States to support England and the allies in their defense measures, short of war. When Roosevelt wrote a letter to Thompson thanking her for this effort, the silence towards MacCracken spoke for itself.

MacCracken was abroad on leave in Europe in the fall of 1922 when George Nettleton, the Yale English professor substituting for him as acting Vassar College president, went to Hyde Park and had, as he said, a "very pleasant talk" with Roosevelt, who had served as Woodrow Wilson's Assistant Secretary of the Navy. Nettleton carried a message from the Vassar board of trustees, asking Roosevelt to join the board as a local trustee. Roosevelt's only hesitation in accepting was whether he would be able to negotiate the board meetings with regularity because of his recently acquired polio, with which he was just learning how to deal. He agreed, nevertheless, to the proposal, and was elected to the board at the February 13, 1923, meeting. Roosevelt continued on the Vassar board through his New York gubernatorial tenure. In 1933, after he had become President, his ten-year trusteeship was due to end in June. The board desired him to stay on as honorary trustee while he was in the White House, however, and extended him the invitation to do so, which he accepted. He was still an honorary trustee when he died at Warm Springs in 1945.

The Roosevelts were from old, conservative, Dutch stock in the Hudson Valley, but their politics were more liberal than most of their fellow residents of Dutchess County, who by and large voted Republican. The future President did have a group of Democratic political associates in the neighborhood, such as Judge John Mack and other prominent local professionals, and later when he came back from Washington, he would count on these people, as well as his Washington aides, to help him negotiate his public appearances in Dutchess County. Speaking from the porch of the president's house or the platform of the chapel, Roosevelt would sometimes use the Vassar campus as his stage.

Soon after FDR joined the board, MacCracken wrote him that he thought he would find the board of trustees "as active and as loyal as any board in the country."[2] This was a big change, MacCracken offered, from the situation eight years before when he himself came in as Vassar president. Then some members of the board still treated the college as "an expensive plaything," he acknowledged. Now in the 1920s, MacCracken wrote, the trustees were a group of men and women characteristically eager to give time and thought to the development of the college. In June 1923—a few months after Roosevelt came on the board—the trustees adopted the Vassar College Statute of Instruction, a new set of collegiate bylaws in which the college was conceived of as an organic institution and the duties and responsibilities of trustees, faculty, administration, and students were clearly set forth. Whereas under Taylor the trustees had engaged in many matters relating to the details of the academic side of the college, that was no longer the case by 1923. The Vassar Governance, as the new constitution was later called, soon became a model for government in academic institutions around the country, as well as defining MacCracken's goals for autonomy at Vassar itself.

In MacCracken's first years, the local trustees, who, in practical terms, tied and untied the purse strings of the college, lived in Poughkeepsie or nearby—John Adriance, Daniel Smiley, H.V. Pelton—and had a free reign in settling the day-to-day matters of the business part of the college. But after 1923, the local trustees ceased operating in that practical role. What MacCracken wanted for the college at that point was the election to the board of someone new whose presence could bring distinction and prominence to the connection. Roosevelt was the choice. Having Roosevelt on the board would draw the college into the affairs of the county, the state, and the nation.

It is not too surprising that MacCracken gravitated towards Roosevelt; they had much in common. They were both Democrats, they were both very community conscious, and each participated in many civic and political activities. Harvard-educated men, they were both quick-witted and had golden tongues. At a deeper level, they were interested in social change, yet steeped in tradition. When they made each other's acquaintance, they must have seen how deeply they were both interested in the history of the county and their part of the country. Both of them early made the acquaintance of Helen Reynolds, a prominent local historian, who presided over the historical research of the Dutchess County Historical Society, of which they were simultaneously on the board. Both of them revelled also in digging up antiquities and connections with the earlier settlers of the past. Roosevelt was an inspired choice, all around, for local Vassar trustee, and in some respects, although not all, was MacCracken's ideological matchmate.

The first assignment given Roosevelt as trustee was an appointment as chairman of a county committee (the other members of which were the warden, the dean, and the president of the Vassar Students' Association), with the task of making plans for a Dutchess County Day at the college.[3] This was a conscious step on the part of the college to become more visible and participatory in local Dutchess County affairs. Around the same time that Roosevelt was tapped as trustee in 1923, Laura Delano, his cousin, was invited to head a committee of local friends of the college "which," MacCracken said, "we desire to form here in the county in order to promote more pleasant social relations and to let our neighbors know more about the work this really unique institution is doing. It seems a great pity that we should go on living together without knowing more about each other."

"The index to Dr. Taylor's Vassar did not contain the word 'Poughkeepsie,'" MacCracken observed after retirement.[4] "If I ever wrote a book about the college, it would be found."

The local newspaper account of the event reported that over two hundred residents of the county visited the college on the first county day in 1924 at the invitation of MacCracken and the trustees. The guests were ushered first into the parlors of Main Building, where they were received by President MacCracken, Dean Thompson, Warden Jean Palmer, and four trustees: Mrs. Minnie Cumnock Blodgett, Mrs. M. J. Allen, Mr. R. G. Guernsey, and Mr. H. V. Pelton. Student guides, acting as hostesses, took the visitors around the campus and to the various halls. At four o'clock, a play, The Under of Wishes, by Hallie Flanagan, soon-to-be Vassar's theatre professor, later to be tapped by Roosevelt for the leadership of the Federal Theatre Program, was given by the students at the outdoor theatre, and after the play, the faculty met the guests at tea in the gallery of Taylor Hall, the elegant new art building, built in 1914.

Because the campus urgently needed a new dormitory to accommodate the mounting numbers of students, the Committee on Buildings, of which Roosevelt was at once made a member, was considering the erection of a new structure in the center of the quadrangle of dormitories and one classroom building, which would be linked to all the existing quadrangle dormitories and would provide a common kitchen for all—an earlier version of the All Campus Dining Center, ACDC, which in 1972 replaced Students Building, the early student center, built in 1913. One hundred and forty students lived off campus in 1923, and this plan would have improved dining facilities and freed rooms for dormitory space. The idea was scuttled when it was decided instead to develop Wing Farm, an area to the northeast end of the campus, and build Cushing House in 1928, along with Blodgett, Kendrick, and the Wimpfheimer Nursery School. During 1924 the Buildings committee voted "their moral obligation to erect Sanders Physics Building." Henry Sanders, chairman of the board earlier in the decade, had left money for that purpose, but the building had been much postponed when the Blodgetts loomed onto the scene with the promise of things to come in the way of an euthenics building. Roosevelt was very interested in these enterprises, and put forth his own ideas as plans were debated. When he couldn't make meetings because of government commitments, he sometimes sent memoranda about his thoughts.

In 1925 trustee Roosevelt was especially concerned that with a rise in tuition the children of professionals—middle class people—would still be able to afford a college education. In his capacity as chair of the Committee on Religious Life, also, he presided over deliberations, which considered making attendance at Vassar Chapel (non-denominational services) voluntary for the first time since the beginning of the college. The idea, promoted by MacCracken, was that the college president would invite the cooperation of faculty and students in planning for the "successful adoption, maintenance, and support of voluntary chapel service." Roosevelt stated that he would hesitate to vote for the abolition of required chapel on Sundays and expressed the view that it would be well to separate the weekday and Sunday questions. The plan, which was finally adopted, catered to his ideas. The trustee minutes specified :

On such Monday evenings as the President may deem advisable, he may summon in assembly the whole of the college, not to last over one-half hour, at the same hour and in the same place. With the exception of a single hymn, such a meeting would not be religious but would be devoted to the consolidation of the ideals of the college. The remaining four days of the week would carry a simple religious service, not differing greatly from the then current service, as conducted by the president.

Those trustee deliberations preceded the acceptance of the idea of voluntary chapel services, and the institution of morning chapel talks given by MacCracken, a custom kept up for many years. (His notes for those talks, ranging in scope from recounting Chaucer's tales to addressing contemporary social activism, constitute one whole box of documents in the MacCracken Papers in Special Collections.) Matthew Vassar had decreed that all sectarian influences should be carefully excluded from his college, but that the "training of …students should never be intrusted to the skeptical, the irreligious, or the immoral." MacCracken's presidential predecessors, all Baptist clergymen stretching back to 1861, had presided over required daily and Sunday chapel services, which some students and faculty, including the astronomer Maria Mitchell, had continuously fretted against even back in the early days. The clergymen presidents had also successively offered a mandatory and solemn presidential course in moral ethics for seniors, a kind of exit-into-life course, pulling together issues of morality. MacCracken was a man of deep religious convictions, but as soon as he became president, he requested from the trustees permission to abolish the ethics course and substitute instead a required course in the philosophy of the liberal arts education, to be offered to freshmen rather than seniors. Consistent with this resecularization of the Vassar educational environment, MacCracken was asked in 1929 to look into procuring a denominational pastor (chaplain) for affiliation with the college, to determine directions that might be followed in connection with campus religious life, but as there was no money in the budget for a new enterprise, he could not implement that idea at that time.

The general question, initiated by MacCracken, of Vassar's

helping William Lawrence to found the experimental junior college Sarah Lawrence came up in 1926, early in Roosevelt's tenure. Certainly in 1926, it was helpful to MacCracken to have Roosevelt on the board as he heartily endorsed and supported the president's forward-looking interest in the Sarah Lawrence collaboration. Later on in 1932, with Roosevelt still active on the board, the Vassar trustees declared themselves as more than pleased with the initial five-year development of Sarah Lawrence and asked MacCracken to continue his relationship as ex officio member of the Sarah Lawrence board.

In 1929 Roosevelt, by then governor of the state of New York, was a member of the first trustee committee on undergraduate life that, among other questions, established permission for students to smoke in particular places on campus. (Later in November it was proposed by the newly formed household management committee of the trustees that the rooms thus set aside for smoking, should be known as "rooms in which students may smoke," not as "smoking rooms." That way, it would be clear that the rooms could be kept under the supervision of the wardens, and that smoking could be controlled.) The governor was also a member of the first trustee endowment committee, which established the need for an assistant to the president to work on money-raising, a move which in turn led to a separate development office in 1929.

On the tenth of June 1931, Roosevelt, then in his second term as governor, delivered the Vassar commencement address. Ahead of time Roosevelt thought it was likely that he might have to miss the commencement, so Stephen Duggan, fellow trustee and head of the Institute of International Education, the I.I.E., agreed to stand in if necessary, in which case he would have given a specially prepared address on "America's Place in International Affairs," an appropriate topic for one who had done so much to promote international education at Vassar and elsewhere. But Roosevelt did turn up, the first governor of a state to deliver a commencement address at Vassar, and gave a short speech on the theme that study is like navigation, liberally illustrated with anecdotes to bring home his point. The speech conveyed the idea that "the crass ignorance of the educated classes about governmental matters [was] one of the most appalling things about the post-war years" and the students were exhorted to do better than the older generation had done to understand what was going on in governmental affairs around them.

Two years later on June 1, 1933, MacCracken proudly reported to the trustees:

> For the first time in the history of Vassar a trustee of the Board has been elected to the highest office in the country. Franklin D. Roosevelt, whose term expires with this meeting, has maintained throughout his connection with the college undiminished interest in its work. While his administrative duties have prevented his attendance at recent meetings, he has been most faithful in personal conferences and in correspondence. The many contacts which the college enjoys both with the President and Mrs. Roosevelt must remain a treasured part of its history.[5]

MacCracken had determined a course of action to keep Roosevelt interested in remaining on the board as an honorary member, however, knowing that his affiliation would continue to lend distinction to the college even if the President didn't have time to do his trustee homework. Thus before Roosevelt's trustee term was up, in April of 1933, MacCracken sent a short but pithy progress report to the White House about how the town-gown projects were going: the students were making surveys for various local agencies and the college was opening its doors more widely to townspeople for concerts, lectures, and forums. Roosevelt was invited to attend commencement, to make his final appearance as active trustee, an invitation which he had to decline. At a board meeting near the time of commencement, however, the trustees unanimously voted to ask him to stay on as honorary trustee, which Roosevelt agreed to do. MacCracken put it this way in his letter of invitation: "Your post was described as carrying with it all the authority you would like to exercise, and none of the responsibility."[6]

After Roosevelt had agreed to stay on the Vassar board, the

MacCrackens gave an August reception for him, to which residents of the county were invited. MacCracken went to Hyde Park to escort Roosevelt to the campus, and joined Roosevelt in his open and specially-equipped car for the ride back. During the ride, Roosevelt gave him a lesson in how to pose for photographs, first greeting people standing on one side of the road as the car went through, and then on the other. Roosevelt said to MacCracken, "You'll learn," the *Poughkeepsie Evening News* dutifully reported on August 26, 1933. MacCracken and Roosevelt were having a wonderful time, each associating with the other, fellow masters of histrionics.

Roosevelt delivered his speech from the MacCracken's front porch, after an introductory greeting by MacCracken who said:

> Mr. President: The people of Dutchess County bid you welcome. You have graciously fulfilled your promise in coming from your vacation days, days that for anyone else would be called hard work, to speak again to your neighbors. A year ago when you spoke to us at Washington Hollow [nearby township], there were whispers in the air, whispers about somebody that was a stranger to us of Dutchess County. He was whispered to be vague. He was thought to be timid. He was rumored to be weak. Worst of all, we heard he was aristocratic. We had never known such a man, and we wondered whom they had considered. Now the rumors and whispers have died away, and a great chorus of praise and pride has filled our ears. A man stands out whom everybody knows. The portrait is more familiar but not even his neighbors knew him last year as the world knows him now. He has taught us to be strong. He has kindled his courage in our own hearts. He has drawn for us a clear and definite plan by which through sacrifice and cooperation, American democracy may survive. And best of all, he has placed human values first, and has affirmed that the state exists for the welfare of all, and not least for the common men and women like his neighbors.

During these Depression years, MacCracken advised Roosevelt from time to time what people in the Vassar community were thinking; he believed that the college might represent a kind of listening post. One sign of recovery from the Depression, for example, he pointed out to Roosevelt by letter in 1934: advance registration for future classes at Vassar from January to July in 1934 was the largest in over ten years, and in 1934 fewer students needed special aid. (The college during the Depression had gone on to a semi-self-help regimen, designed to cut down on college and student expenditures. Some students maintained their own quarters and did their own housekeeping, and a cooperative house was established, at first in euthenics quarters in Blodgett Hall, in which students also did their own purchasing and cooking.)

In 1935 when Harry Hopkins, the old childhood and Grinnell College friend of Hallie Flanagan, drew Roosevelt's attention to her as a promising candidate for the directorship of the Federal Theatre program (part of the Federal Emergency Relief program), MacCracken lost, at least temporarily, an outstandingly innovative faculty member and one who had already brought great liveliness to the Vassar community as director of the Vassar Experimental Theatre. By that time the Vassar theatre had come into national prominence. Eleanor Roosevelt had attended some of Hallie's lively interdisciplinary Living Newspaper plays, which explored serious contemporary issues and experienced their excitement. When Hallie travelled to Washington at Hopkins' invitation to consider heading the program, Eleanor supported her for the position.

When Roosevelt was reelected in 1936, MacCracken sent him a telegram saying: "Our cup runneth over," to which Roosevelt replied: "Dear Henry: That is a mighty sweet note of yours."

Yet, as indicated above, everything was not entirely harmonious between MacCracken and FDR, as World War II approached. In May 1940 seventy-five Vassar College students signed a letter to FDR protesting that they did not agree with him on the war-peace question with regard to the United States' role in the European conflict. MacCracken's own stand on American involvement in World War II was in direct conflict with FDR's foreign policy— which he often explicitly criticized. Although in February 1941, and again in April of the same year, he declined to join the America First organization (with which he was flirting because its philosophy of non-intervention approached his own), MacCracken gave several speeches and made many public statements that year in keeping with his pacifism, endorsing a non-interventionist policy.

In August 1941 MacCracken gave such a speech at Carnegie Hall, after which FDR made it immediately clear that he disapproved strongly of American isolationists, pacifists, and non-interventionists. After FDR announced in September 1941 that United States ships would fire upon threatening Axis ships, MacCracken appeared before the Senate Foreign Relations Committee to testify against the proposed changes to the 1939 Neutrality Act, which would allow American ships to be armed. Pearl Harbor sharply ended MacCracken's involvement in the anti-war movement, but Roosevelt and MacCracken did not thereafter resume their former cordial relationship.

Dean C. Mildred Thompson, on the other hand, was very openly in favor of Roosevelt's policies during the same period. The two administrators had to agree to disagree over this issue, which provoked some strain between them. When one hundred and twenty-five faculty members wrote a letter to Roosevelt in October 1941 pledging their support of his foreign policy, Mildred Thompson sought to soothe MacCracken's anguish by sending a formal note to her colleague, of whom she was genuinely fond, in advance:

> My dear President MacCracken,
>
> With a sense of courtesy and respect for you, and in understanding of your genuine belief in the right of free expression, both within the college and without, we wish you to have a copy of our statement of public policy before it goes to the President of the United States, and before it may appear in the press.
>
> We feel sure you will receive this statement in the spirit of tolerance for different opinions which you have long shown and which we greatly value.…
>
> —Mildred Thompson[7]

Roosevelt's easy interaction on many occasions with individuals and groups of people in MacCracken's and Thompson's Vassar, especially in the thirties and forties, awakened many students, and even faculty members, trustees and parents, to politics and national affairs, to taking sides and thinking for themselves on issues of war and peace, and the unsolved Depression problems of hunger, homelessness, and unemployment.

MacCracken's arm, reaching out into the community to bring outsiders in, and his knack for encouraging students both inside and outside classrooms, to become engaged with the developments of their own times, were nowhere more observable than in the college's give-and-take relationship with the Roosevelts. For some students, indeed, the opportunity to meet or just hear from a local platform, Eleanor and Franklin Roosevelt, and discover how they thought, presented themselves, listened and got things done, constituted the essence of experiential learning, which was the fulcrum of MacCracken's theory of education. For at least one student, who grew up during the Depression years, subjected to conservative parental fulminations against the "country squire in the White House," the chance to get an entirely different slant on the Roosevelts, showing their sides as concerned educators, county citizens and neighbors, proved MacCracken's point.

NOTES

1. Franklin D. Roosevelt to Henry N. MacCracken, Henry Noble MacCracken Papers, Box 2, Vassar College Archives.
2. Henry Noble MacCracken Papers, Box 72, Vassar College Archives.
3. Ibid.
4. Henry Noble MacCracken Papers, Box 120, Vassar College Archives.
5. Roosevelt's Board Service, Vassar College Trustee Minutes, Vassar College Archives, Box 3, passim.
6. President's personal files, Franklin Delano Roosevelt Archives, 108, FDR Library.
7. C. Mildred Thompson File, FDR Papers, Franklin Delano Roosevelt Archives, FDR Library.

Three Memoirs of F.D.R.

The three articles that follow were written by women who were born, grew up in Hyde Park and who share an interest in local history. All have served as President of the Town of Hyde Park Historical Society at different times, and all have served the town in their work and/or volunteer activities. The articles by Margaret Marquez and Patsy Costello are based on their reminiscences. Diane Lobb-Boyce's knowledge of Top Cottage is an integral part of her work for the National Park Service.

F.D.R. in Hyde Park

Margaret Marquez

Franklin Delano Roosevelt came into the world at Hyde Park on January 30, 1882. As his father said, he was a big baby: "He weighed 10 pounds without any clothes." Fortunately for him he was born into two aristocratic families whose estates along the Hudson River he learned to love. His parents provided a protective childhood and much parental companionship. While still quite young, Franklin had his own pony and rode daily with his father, a breeder of horses. Children of neighbors were his playmates—Archie Rogers, Jr., and his brother, Edmond, as well as Mary Newbold, who lived next door. Franklin and the Rogers children shared a tutor at "Crumwold," the Rogers' home. They were outdoor youngsters with common interests. They liked sailing homemade boats, learning about animals, and digging tunnels in the snow. When Franklin was a little older his father taught him to sail the yacht at Campobello, their summer home, and to race an iceboat on the frozen Hudson. In winter there was also skating on the ice pond and tobogganing down the woods road toward the river. He learned to swim when he was young and rowing soon followed. Good manners were taught and insisted upon by both parents. Despite not having siblings, his childhood was a happy one.

At fourteen Franklin was enrolled in a strict private school,

Margaret Logan Marquez was born and brought up in Hyde Park. She is the author of Hyde Park on the Hudson *(Arcadia Press, 1996), now in its second edition. For eight years she was the Town of Hyde Park Historian. Her sources are a lifetime of acquaintance with members of the Roosevelt family, and her own interest in the town's history.*

Groton, outside Boston. There he had to learn to be one of a group, and although he often felt left out he never complained to his parents. The son of Franklin's half-brother was also enrolled at the school and this caused Franklin much embarrassment, as Taddy did not behave properly. Franklin was not a great athlete and was an average student. After Groton, he went on to Harvard, where many of his courses dealt with government. Unfortunately, Taddy followed him and created the same problems of misconduct. While at Harvard, Franklin's father died, and this caused a great void for him as they had been lifetime companions.

Franklin, at eighteen, felt himself responsible for his mother, although she had been named his guardian and was quite capable of handling her life as well as his. At the same time his cousin, Theodore Roosevelt, was running for Vice President with William McKinley and this was a source of pride to FDR. He cast his first vote in Hyde Park, a custom he followed the rest of his life. During his years at Harvard he renewed his acquaintance with a distant female cousin, Eleanor Roosevelt, who had returned from a private school in England and was doing social work in New York City. After graduating from Harvard he entered Columbia Law School to be near her. Although his mother thought they were too young, Franklin and Eleanor were married on Saint Patrick's Day, 1905, with President Theodore Roosevelt giving his niece in marriage.

Franklin and Eleanor spent the first week of their marriage at Springwood in Hyde Park. During the next several years Franklin practiced law in New York City, was elected to office in the New York State Senate, and later appointed Assistant Secretary of the Navy, all of which involved several moves. The family returned to Springwood as often as possible. When nominated as Vice President with James Cox in 1920, the ceremonies took place at Springwood, not the usual site of political rallies. The house had been enlarged to make room for Franklin and Eleanor's growing family. At the time he was a partner in the law firm of Carter, Ledyard and Millburn in New York City. Weekdays were spent in New York and weekends at Springwood; summer vacations were spent at Campobello. It was there during the summer of 1921 that FDR was stricken with paralyzing polio.

Sara Delano Roosevelt was convinced Franklin should be a country squire, albeit in a wheelchair, while Eleanor and political strategist Louis Howe were just as determined he should be a productive individual. For seven years he divided his time between the New York City house and Springwood, using crutches, braces, canes and a friendly arm to support him. He spent hours on crutches trying to walk from the Hyde Park house to the main gate, always hoping to gain the use of his legs. He also spent much time at Warm Springs, Georgia, exercising his legs in the healthful waters. He made his first public appearance in 1924 at the nomination of Al Smith for President in Madison Square Garden. At the 1928 presidential election he again nominated Al Smith. That same year FDR was himself nominated for and won the election of Governor of New York State. There followed the presidential elections of 1932, 1936, 1940 and 1944. He again returned to Hyde Park as often as possible. According to the National Park Service, FDR came back to Springwood at least 135 times during his 12 years as President.

The visits to Hyde Park connected him with local people, about whom he knew a great deal. He treated everyone equally, believing each person had value. He worked with Col. Archibald Rogers in reforestation, both at Springwood and later on land he acquired that became known as Val-Kill. Some of the Val-Kill plantings were later sold as Christmas trees by his son, Elliott. His tenant farmer, Moses Smith, was visited regularly for information, advice, and the latest town news. Another source of information was Ben Haviland, whom he called "Uncle Benny," the Town Historian before Franklin was named to that post. (FDR gave it up when he became Governor.) Hyde Park was a special place for FDR. He was really very interested in town and county history, His collection of material at the presidential library testifies to those interests. Even while he was President and involved in a world war, FDR still gathered local material to be saved for future use.

FDR's father instilled in him the importance of taking part

in local affairs. James had been Town Supervisor at one point. As a school trustee, he made monthly visits to check on teachers and conditions. Franklin held his father's horse while he visited classes in the Hyde Park Union Free School. When, in 1927, Sara Roosevelt decided to give a public library to the village in memory of her husband, Franklin assisted her in selecting the location and drawing plans. Following a family tradition, there was a party on Christmas afternoons for those who worked on the estate, and FDR was always there to greet them. The workers admired him for his knowledge about the estate and enjoyed his kindness and good sense of humor.

Old time residents of Hyde Park, who had always known FDR, did not think of him as a politician but as a friendly neighbor. He often drove around town in his hand-operated blue Ford and, seeing someone on the street whom he knew, he stopped to talk. The villagers, mostly Republicans, told each other how much they liked him and what he was doing, but they would not change their ballots to vote for him. Once a Republican, always a Republican, even if a well-liked local man was running for President of the United States! That was the way it was. After the ballots were counted elsewhere and it was clear he had won, a torchlight parade was formed and a large group marched down the Post Road to Springwood to congratulate him with torches made of wads of material dipped in oil. FDR was familiar with the tradition and he and the family would be on the front porch to greet the group. One night he told them, "I am glad to see you all. I know you didn't vote for me, but I am glad to see you anyway."

Hyde Park was a place where FDR relaxed and became a regular citizen. He was interested in everything local. He joined the fraternal organization of Odd Fellows and was a member of the fire company. He attended games of the local baseball team, the "Robin Hoods," and served as a vestryman and senior warden at St. James Episcopal Church. When the Methodist Church celebrated its 100th anniversary, he was the guest speaker. While his mother lived, the menus at Springwood revolved around his likes. He had a healthy appetite and enjoyed a cocktail. Food prepared by the Scotch cook was bought from the Hyde Park butcher. He took visiting royalty to local churches—the King and Queen of England to St. James Church in 1939, and Princess Juliana of Holland to the Reformed Dutch Church when she came in 1941. Before FDR became Governor, he asked some local people to establish a Democratic Club, despite the town and county being powerfully Republican. The Roosevelt Home Club was the result. The birthday celebrations it sponsored for FDR eventually became the March of Dimes. Every summer there were gatherings at Woodlawns, the home of Mr. and Mrs. Moses Smith. The West Point Band played at these events and the President spoke about what was going on in Washington. During the war, whenever European royalty were visiting they would attend this event with FDR and Mrs. Roosevelt.

While FDR was President he was protected by both the Secret Service and a company of Military Police stationed in Hyde Park. These soldiers were housed on the Rogers Estate and the Secret Service in the Vanderbilt Mansion. Small guardhouses were located at every entrance to the estates and throughout the woods and on rooftops. Seeing military trucks and personnel was common in the area then. In order to conceal the identity of leaders during the war the names of estate employees were given to them.

FDR hoped to return to Hyde Park to live when his term of office was over. His stated wish to go back to his home on the Hudson River, expressed his desire to continue working on local history and making the farm a profitable operation. In keeping with his affection for Hyde Park and Springwood, he established the nation's first presidential library. Recognizing that his papers would be used in the future, he located the library and museum to form a complex with his home and burial site. By doing so, he made Hyde Park an international center of interest for the world.

The F.D.R. Home Club

Patsy Newman Costello

My knowledge of the Franklin D. Roosevelt Home Club stems in part from memories of my parents' involvement in the Club. It is documented in a collection of newspaper articles, photographs and other memorabilia in my possession, and in part from my own experience as a teenager.

In late 1928, after his election as Governor of New York State, Franklin Roosevelt met with Hyde Parkers Everetta Killmer and Erden Ackert and asked them to organize a group of supporters into a political club. A delegation made preparations to go to Albany on January 1, 1929 for the gubernatorial inauguration and to take part in the parade as the "Club from Hyde Park." Approximately forty local supporters went to Albany by bus, arriving in a snowstorm for the festivities. Later that month the Home Club was officially formed as a group of local citizens dedicated to promoting interest in FDR. Bylaws were drafted and approved by members. Organized at first as a local Democratic Club, the Home Club soon became nonpartisan, open to all who wished to join. People from every state, as well as Canada and Puerto Rico, became members of the Home Club. At one time the membership reached 1500.

During FDR's governorship and presidency the Club met regularly and members were active in local politics. They often met

Patsy Newman Costello is a native of Hyde Park and has lived in the same house on Main Street all of her life. Ms. Costello graduated from the Katharine Gibbs School in Providence, R.I. and worked at the I.B.M. Corporation for several years. She is the current President of the Town of Hyde Park Historical Society and serves on the Board of Trustees of the Hyde Park Free Library.

FDR's train when he returned to Hyde Park from Washington, D.C. and other destinations. They went to "Springwood" to learn where he had been and what was going on in the world. Club members also traveled to Albany and Washington to show their support. They attended two gubernatorial inaugurations in Albany and four inaugurals in Washington. An article in *The Knickerbocker Press* on June 12, 1930 reported that more than 100 members of the Home Club took a day trip to Albany to visit their neighbor:

> "Most of them, who either knew the Governor since childhood or were known to him since their childhood, were greeted personally at the Executive Chamber. The Governor sat in the big chair of his private office on the second floor of the Capitol as the group marched in and shook hands, one by one. Hardly any escaped being greeted by their first names, whether they were little girls in short dresses or the elders of the party, some of whom recalled incidents of the Governor's boyhood at Hyde Park."

My parents, Alton and Margaret Newman, as well as my grandmother and aunts, attended the Presidential Inauguration in 1937, and later in May, a buffet dinner at the White House. I remember my mother telling me they stayed at the Mayflower Hotel, which is still in operation today. Annual Birthday Ball celebrations in honor of the President were held in Hyde Park.

The Home Club continued after President Roosevelt died in 1945. My mother, Margaret Andros Newman, was its president from the late 1950s until her death in 1961. I was a member as well and, as a teenager, I went to teas at Val-Kill after Memorial Day services in the Rose Garden. My mother introduced many noted speakers at these services, and I still have copies of the programs. I was a guest with my mother at several teas. I remember Mrs. Roosevelt personally serving homemade ice cream to her guests at the end of the table. In addition to all the cakes, pies and cookies, she gave us a choice of vanilla or chocolate ice cream.

The Home Club sponsored several card parties that were held

on the lawn at Val-Kill. They were fundraisers for Club activities, and many local people enjoyed an afternoon of playing cards and games. After refreshments, Mrs. Roosevelt spoke to the group telling us of her recent visits around the world. After Mrs. Roosevelt's death in 1962, there was less interest in the Home Club and it finally disbanded in 1975.

Club ribbon.
P. N. COSTELLO

Eleanor Roosevelt loved violets. In the 1930s and 40s, Dutchess County was known as the violet capitol and there were many greenhouses in Hyde Park, Rhinebeck and Red Hook. It was a tradition whenever Home Club members went to Washington to take her violets from Dutchess County. When a group of Hyde Parkers went to Washington, D.C. in 1997 to attend the FDR Memorial Dedication, they continued the tradition by bringing two wreaths of violets to place at the Memorial, one for Eleanor and one for Franklin.

BIBLIOGRAPHY

The Roosevelt Home Club Papers, 1929-1975, FDR Library, Hyde Park, NY

Killmer, Evaretta, "Recollections of the Franklin D. Roosevelt Home Club, Hyde Park, NY," FDR Library, Hyde Park, NY

Letter from Eleanor Roosevelt to Mr. McIntyre, dated May 10, 1937, on the Roosevelt Home Club coming for a buffet supper on May 29, 1937, FDR Library, Hyde Park, NY

Top Cottage

Diane Lobb-Boyce

" . . . to escape the mob . . ."1
Franklin Delano Roosevelt

If walls could talk…. Today Top Cottage sits in silence off a road at the end of a development. It is a monument to a president long gone from the world we live in today. The presidency, with all its glory, hopes and disappointments, has to be one of the biggest burdens one human being can carry. Regardless of advisors, supporters, family and friends, there is no vacation from the office. The job is, in today's vernacular, 24/7. Franklin Delano Roosevelt, the President of the United States and a native of Dutchess County, knew that only too well.

As an adult, FDR was to say that until he was seven years old, "Hyde Park was the center of my life." In many ways that remained true all his life. His devotion to his roots in the Hudson Valley were deep and strong no matter where the tide took him. He left the Hudson Valley at the age of fourteen to attend private school in Groton, Massachusetts. He then went on to Harvard University and to law school at Columbia University in New York City. Wherever he was, the house on the bluff overlooking the Hudson was home.

Diane Lobb-Boyce is a native of Hyde Park. She graduated from local schools and Dutchess Community College, with a concentration in Political Science and History. From 1985 to 1995 she was the Town of Hyde Park Historian. For the past 23 years, she has worked for the National Park Service at the Roosevelt-Vanderbilt National Historic Sites. As an interpreter, she was chosen to research, develop and train staff for Top Cottage.

The Roosevelt home was named "Springwood" in the early 1880s by James and Sara Roosevelt. FDR's interest in his home environs was nurtured at home from the time of his birth. His father, James, (1828-1900), professed a great fondness for country life and often introduced himself to strangers as: "I'm James Roosevelt and I have a farm at Hyde Park," as though people meeting him anywhere in his travels would know where Hyde Park, New York was. Sara shared his affection for the countryside and often referred to their home as "dear Hyde Park." Using the name of their estate interchangeably with the small village that grew up amidst several estates created confusion about the place that continues to this day.

For young FDR the freedom of country life, the stability of his parents, and the daily rounds of the property with his father gave him a sense of place, a purpose in life. His father receives little recognition for all that he taught his young son in the few years they had together. James Roosevelt died when FDR was only 18 years old, and in his first year at Harvard. A graduate of Union College in Schenectady, NY and of Harvard Law School, James left a clause in his will that his wife, "should forever be responsible for Franklin." Sara Roosevelt took that seriously, giving their son the great confidence that made him a player on the world stage. It is from these roots that the story of his retreat, "Top Cottage," as a place "to escape the mob" comes.

Top Cottage

It began when FDR was elected to the presidency in 1932. He had such good relationships with his family, friends and neighbors that even though he had just become President of the United States, they felt no qualms about coming down his driveway and showing up at the door to discuss issues as important as the Depression and as local as who should be on the Vestry of the St. James Episcopal Church. FDR himself encouraged this informality by driving around the county in his specially rigged Ford, popping up at the edge of a neighbor's driveway or tooling along country roads. He

At Top Cottage: FDR and Ruthie Bie with Fala. FDR PRESIDENTIAL LIBRARY

was a familiar sight. Early on, however, he recognized that he was not going to be able to be as accessible as he had been.

FDR maintained a lifelong interest in the buildings and surroundings of Hyde Park. He acquired land and oversaw the construction of buildings in the vernacular style of his Dutch antecedents. He wasn't very fussy about how the buildings looked on the inside but he wanted them to look Dutch on the outside. Today, a ramble around Hyde Park will prove that point.

In 1911 he purchased a farm on the edge of the Fallkill Creek on the eastern edge of Route 9G. It was the first property he purchased of his own and was to be used as a forestry project, something he had become very interested in by the time he arrived in Albany as a fledgling State Senator in 1911. He purchased a second farm in 1924 for a reason beyond the tree plantations. He wanted some recreational space for his large family in addition to the main house on Route 9. The story is told today at the Eleanor Roosevelt National Historic Site that, while picnicking at the site, Mrs. Roosevelt and some friends spoke of regretting they could not return there until Spring as there was no refuge on the property to get out of the elements. FDR offered to build them a cottage and, subsequently, he contacted Henry Toombs, a relative of Caroline O'Day, an associate of Mrs. Roosevelt in the Democratic Party and a partner with mutual friends Nancy Cook and Marion Dickerman.

This marked the beginning of a deep relationship between Roosevelt and Toombs. Together, they designed a small stone cottage on the banks of the Fallkill Creek for "my missus and some of her friends." They now had a place to go in bad weather and in 1926 the cottage, known as "Val-Kill" was completed. That same year Toombs was hired by Sara Delano Roosevelt to build a library in the village of Hyde Park in memory of her late husband. It was constructed in the same style as Val-Kill Cottage, using local fieldstone. The Hyde Park Free Library stands today on the corner of Main Street and U.S. Route 9.

FDR was invited in 1924 to visit a local spa at Warm Springs, Georgia. After having visited there for several years to ease his polio affliction, FDR established the Warm Springs Foundation in 1927, He hired Henry Toombs to build what is today the small cottage that meant as much to FDR as his home in Hyde Park and the family summer home at Campobello Island. That year Mr. Toombs also completed a small project, re-doing the room at Springwood, which became FDR's study.

Election to the Presidency

When FDR was elected to the presidency in 1932, he assumed office at a difficult time in the nation's history. Land was eroding faster than anyone could imagine; the Depression gripped the countryside; money woes were worldwide and foreign war clouds developed daily. In the minds of many people, FDR went to Washington as the only one who could pull the United States out of the mess.

By 1932, FDR had an ever-growing friendship with a cousin, Margaret Suckley. Known in the family as "Daisy," she was eleven years younger than FDR, a spinster lady taking care of an elderly aunt. Ten years earlier she had been formally asked by Sara Delano Roosevelt to keep FDR company as he recovered from polio, but their deep, abiding friendship really began with the 1932 election.

In August 1935, Daisy wrote to FDR that some redwood trees had arrived for planting. The following month she and FDR took a ride to the top of Dutchess Hill. It is a high hill about 400 feet above the Hudson River and approximately two miles due east of the Roosevelt Home. They began to refer to it as "our hill." After FDR's election to a second term in 1936, he became more serious about building some form of retreat away from Springwood. He had planned to find a spot to build not far from the main house. Although not proven to this day, legend has it that his mother did not want him to spend his nights there. She felt he had a perfectly good home to come to each evening. As far as any of the Roosevelt scholars know, he never did stay overnight there. FDR started working with Daisy on a simple design for a "lean-to," just something to get out of the elements, with perhaps a kitchen area to store items needed for his use when he was there. He began to think of it in terms of a daytime retreat. He planned, once he had finished his second term, to use the cottage on a daily basis, returning to Springwood at night. At that time, he had no idea of being elected to a third or even a fourth term. He began to design a house with Daisy. They were kindred spirits and they could, as Daisy later said, talk to each other about everything and anything. By October 1935, they were exchanging plans and sketches of what he wanted to have at the cottage.

In April 1936, FDR purchased the Rohan Farm, which contained 122 acres, including a ridgeline where the cottage would be built. Daisy and FDR drove there often. They exchanged letters and ideas and even bought books for the cottage. In 1938, FDR sketched a formal plan for the cottage and sent it to Henry Toombs. What had begun as a simple lean-to, to escape the mob, was turning into a formal cottage of several rooms.

FDR and Toombs drew up specific plans: FDR wanted a large living room, a downstairs bedroom, and a small, service-like kitchen with no immediate plans for a refrigerator or stove. He wanted to use local fieldstone for the outside walls but he had already "raided" the stone wall fences on 1600 acres of property, most of which still belonged to his mother. By July 1938, the excavation was almost finished. The service systems—heat, ductwork and other construction - were moving along. FDR was pleased with the progress. By fall, the electrical work was being discussed. In the spring of 1939 most of the cottage work was completed and FDR brought furniture to the cottage. Refinements in construction and changes to various systems would occur over the next two years. On April 14, 1939 it was ready to use.

"If the Walls Could Talk"

On the May 1, 1939 the first visitors had lunch on the west porch. They were the Crown Prince and Princess of Denmark. The next royal visit was the one that is still talked about. On June 11, 1939, King George VI and his wife, Queen Elizabeth, came to Hyde Park to visit President and Mrs. Roosevelt. It was during this visit that the famous "hot dog picnic" occurred, and the American press became indignant when they learned Mrs. Roosevelt was going to serve hot dogs to royalty. What has been left out of the accounts is that they were also served many other American specialties: smoked turkey, Kentucky ham, and strawberry shortcake. It turned out to be a spectacular event in the eyes of the press and the American and English people. It grounded FDR and the King to the coming struggle of World War II. There are still people who talk about the event today as though it had just occurred. Shortly before the death of the Queen Mother in 2002, she allowed the story to be told about fearing for the lives of the King and herself on the way to the picnic as they were being driven up a very steep road by the President himself.

After that picnic there followed 100 or more visits by FDR with various family members, friends, political associates and presidential aides. For FDR, the draw was that he could invite anyone he wanted, leaving behind those he did not want for whatever reason. He delighted in going to Top Cottage for as short a time as one hour or for as long as half a day. Picnic hampers of food from the main house, including FDR's particular favorite sandwich of egg salad and mustard greens, followed Roosevelt in his little Ford to be enjoyed later on the porch.

There were accommodations for the wheelchair. FDR had the mind of an inventor. It was one way he coped with his polio. At Top Cottage he had an outside earth berm built on the north side of the cottage porch. He could drive his car through the woods from the Roosevelt home, through the Val-Kill property and up a primitive road, to Top Cottage. He was able to get into his wheelchair and roll himself off the berm onto the porch. The wheelchair would be taken away as he got himself into a piece of porch furniture. He took great delight in preparing tea and toast for his guests. Daisy often said "you never had toast so good as what had been buttered by the President of the United States!" Perhaps later in the day a table set up alongside his chair allowed FDR to mix cocktails himself.

FDR spent many happy hours on that porch. Springtime was one of his greatest pleasures. He liked to arrive in Hyde Park in time to see the dogwoods blooming in the woods. He didn't want foundation plantings or a mowed lawn—he felt it should be informal and "rough."

The Changes

On April 12, 1945, during the closing days of World War II, Franklin Delano Roosevelt died at another of his beloved properties—Warm Springs, Georgia. He had been working on a speech to be delivered at the founding of the United Nations (a term he coined) in San Francisco. For Daisy, the tragedy was the personal loss of a perfect friend.

In the next few weeks Eleanor Roosevelt began to settle the family wills and accounts. A Roosevelt son, Elliott, moved into Top Cottage with his wife, actress Faye Emerson, and began to make some changes from what had been a daytime retreat to a livable year-round home. He left most of the furnishings in place and enclosed the west porch. By 1950, however, Elliott and Faye had divorced. A year later Eleanor and Elliott held a large auction of Roosevelt articles at the Hammer Galleries in New York City. By December 1952, the cottage and surrounding property had been sold to Philip S. Potter, Sr., of Poughkeepsie, New York. For the next forty-four years it would belong to three generations of Potters.

Top Cottage Today

In the mid-1990s it was rumored that the Potters were seriously attempting to sell the cottage. The news filtered down through the National Park Service and the facilities manager, Henry van Brookhoven, contacted members of the Roosevelt family: Kate Roosevelt Whitney, a daughter of James Roosevelt, and Christopher duPont Roosevelt, a son of Franklin Roosevelt, Jr., became involved in the efforts to obtain Top Cottage. They were joined by J. Winthrop Aldrich, Jr., then Deputy Commissioner for Historic Preservation at the New York State Office of Parks, Recreation and Historic Preservation. It took time but their interest and influence as well as the support of organizations behind them, managed to strike a deal with Owen Potter to preserve this piece of American history. In May 1996, he sold the cottage to the Beaverkill Conservancy, an affiliate of the Open Space Institute, and they in turn leased the property to the Franklin and Eleanor Roosevelt Institute.

Surely FDR himself would be pleased at the effort it took to acquire Top Cottage. Today the partnership of the Franklin and Eleanor Roosevelt Institute, the National Park Service, and the Roosevelt family presents a unique and different program for the visiting public at this site. Top Cottage is open from May through

October, Thursdays through Mondays. A shuttle bus from the Presidential home and library provides transportation and visitors are taken on a guided tour through the south end of Hyde Park, across the countryside and up Dutchess Hill to the cottage. An active furnishings committee is hard at work choosing fabrics and some pieces of furniture. At Top Cottage tour groups walk through rooms where the President took his solace. After looking at photographs taken by cousin Daisy, visitors move to the west porch which overlooks a huge piece of the Hudson River viewshed just as did FDR and his distinguished guests, which included Winston Churchill, Admiral Leahy, FDR's press secretary, William Hassett, family members and close friends. The site offers visitors an opportunity to know Franklin Roosevelt in a way that is different from the interpretation of his life and times at Springwood. No one wants to leave the porch.

The sweep of landscape is a catalyst for all manner of conversations and no topic is forbidden. Many questions come forward: Did FDR know about Pearl Harbor, the Holocaust? Why did he allow the Japanese Internment on the West Coast? Did he really have love affairs with other women? Visitors are amazed to hear that Eleanor and Sara Roosevelt came to Top Cottage for picnics and visits. They are surprised to know there were no telephones there and that FDR drove around Hyde Park with minimum Secret Service protection. People find it hard to understand the amount of freedom he had in those days compared to what a president has today. In this setting, visitors make friends with each other and talk about their lives with total strangers. Almost all visitors over the age of fifty-five have some sort of Roosevelt story to tell. One of the most vivid ones was told recently by a man in his sixties in a wheelchair. He explained that he had been a patient at Warm Springs, Georgia because of polio he contracted when he was eighteen years old. He told his story simply, speaking of his treatment and what FDR's struggle had meant to him, and when he finished he thanked us for listening. There wasn't a dry eye on the porch; the tears came for this man's understanding of all that Top Cottage had meant to

FDR. There have been similar stories but none as poignant as his. There is something in the air at Top Cottage and on that porch which makes the whole experience special. Everyone feels it and it is with regret that they leave.

We extend the spirit of the visit with a tour through the north and middle ends of the village. We point out the former F.D. Roosevelt High School, now a middle school named after Benjamin Haviland, a local farmer and dear friend of FDR's who shared his love of local history. Visitors are intrigued by the fact that FDR had great input into the design of the native fieldstone building in the Dutch Colonial style. The first class graduated from that building in 1941. The bus passes Val-Kill, showing visitors how FDR made the drive over "cross lots" from the Roosevelt home through the Val-Kill property and up Dutchess Hill to Top Cottage. We show them the Post Office, the Town Library, the Hyde Park Elementary School, all buildings that have the stamp of FDR. It puts Hyde Park, Springwood and Top Cottage in perspective for them. Now a not-so-well known site becomes the linchpin in the telling of the story of Franklin Roosevelt's hometown, Hyde Park.

1. John G. Waite Associates and Architects, "The President as Architect, Franklin D. Roosevelt's Top Cottage," (Albany, NY, Mount Ida Press, 2001.

BIBLIOGRAPHY

Geoffrey C. Ward, *Before the Trumpet, Young Franklin Delano Roosevelt, 1882-1905*, (New York, NY, Harper and Row Publishers, 1985).

Doris Kearns Goodwin, *No Ordinary Time, Franklin and Eleanor Roosevelt: The Home Front in World War II*, New York, NY, Simon & Schuster, 1994.

Geoffrey C. Ward, Editor and Compiler, *Closest Companion, The Unknown Story of the Intimate Friendship between Franklin Roosevelt and Margaret Suckley*, Houghton Mifflin Company, 1995.

Sara Delano Roosevelt's Diaries, Transcribed and Originals, (Volume I, March 18, 1905) FDR Library, Hyde Park, NY

In-House National Park Services Materials: "Franklin D. Roosevelt's Top Cottage: Historic Furnishing Report," (draft), Nina Gray and Pamela Herrick, 2001; "Historic Structure Report: "The Home of Franklin D. Roosevelt," Peggy Albee, National Park Service, 1989; "Tour of Top Cottage, Village of Hyde Park," developed, researched, & written by Park Ranger Diane Lobb-Boyce.

Roosevelt and His Library

Cynthia M. Koch and Lynn A. Bassanese

The year 1941 is remembered for Pearl Harbor, Lend Lease, Hitler's invasion of the USSR, the Atlantic Charter, and Roosevelt's Four Freedoms Speech. It is also a watershed date in the history of the presidency: on June 30 of that year Franklin D. Roosevelt dedicated his Library in Hyde Park and forever changed the way our nation cares for and preserves the papers of its presidents.

Until Roosevelt, presidents leaving office routinely took their papers with them. George Washington set the precedent in 1797 when he took his files home with him to Mount Vernon with the hope—never fulfilled—of building a library to house them; years later his nephew Bushrod Washington expressed regret that Washington's papers had been "excessively mutilated by Rats."[1] Some former presidents destroyed their papers; others disposed of them

Cynthia M. Koch is Director of the Franklin D. Roosevelt Presidential Library and Museum in Hyde Park, New York. From 1997 through 1999 Dr. Koch was Associate Director of the Penn National Commission on Society, Culture and Community, a research group at the University of Pennsylvania, fostering productive public discourse in American society and abroad. She was Executive Director of the New Jersey Council for the Humanities from 1993 to 1997; from 1979 until 1993 Dr. Koch was director of the Old Barracks Museum, a National Historic Landmark, in Trenton, New Jersey. She holds a Ph.D. and a M.A. in American Civilization from the University of Pennsylvania and a B.A. in History from Pennsylvania State University. Lynn Bassanese is the Director of Public Programs at the Franklin D. Roosevelt Presidential Library and Museum in Hyde Park, New York. She received her B.A. in History from Marist College and has been at the Library since 1972.

haphazardly, making research and study difficult if not impossible. Ulysses S. Grant lost many of his and most of Zachary Taylor's burned when Union troops occupied his son's home in Louisiana in 1862. Chester A. Arthur saw to it himself, setting three garbage cans full of documents on fire the day before his death in 1886.[2]

There were some government attempts to gather the papers —first by the State Department, which eventually acquired the papers of Washington, Jefferson and Madison through the federal appropriations process. The shortcomings of this method grew obvious when the purchase of Madison's papers became embroiled in politics.[3] At the turn of the twentieth century, the families of former presidents began to donate their papers to the Library of Congress, which eventually acquired the earlier papers from the State Department. By the late 1930s it held the bulk of what remained of the papers of twenty-three former presidents. In the meantime a great many presidential papers had disappeared: given away as souvenirs, destroyed, lost in family attics, and sold to autograph collectors.

Another alternative for presidential papers—and one that provided a good precedent for Roosevelt's plan—housed the manuscripts of Rutherford B. Hayes along with the books and mementos of his family at the Hayes Memorial Library in Fremont, Ohio. The holdings were left as a trust and preserved in much the same way FDR planned to preserve his own. The major difference was scale; the Hayes Memorial Library holdings number about 120,000 pages while the Roosevelt Library contains over 17 million pages of archival materials.

Franklin Roosevelt's reasons for building his Library were both personal and public. By 1938 he had accumulated a vast quantity of paper: correspondence, historical manuscripts, books and memorabilia. He was not planning to run for a third term and contemplated retiring to Hyde Park to work on his papers and his collections. On the most basic level he needed a place to house them.

It seemed to friends and family that FDR collected everything:

more than a million stamps in 150 matching albums, 1200 naval prints and paintings, more than 200 fully rigged ship models, 15,000 books. No existing institution, not even the Library of Congress, had room for it all and FDR could not bear to think of breaking it up. Mindful of the size and unusual scope of his collections, he admitted, "Future historians will curse as well as praise me."4

Roosevelt also had the public interest in mind. In erecting his Library, he self-consciously created an historical research institution of unparalleled value and a museum to educate the general public about the Roosevelt years. On 30 June 1941, the President opened the Library with these words:

> The dedication of a library is in itself an act of faith. To bring together the records of the past and to house them in buildings where they will be preserved for the use of men and women in the future, a nation must believe in three things. It must believe in the past. It must believe in the future. It must, above all, believe in the capacity of its own people so to learn from the past that they can gain in judgment in creating their own future.5

The Plan for the Library

Roosevelt studied the problem from every angle before reaching the decision to carve out a sixteen-acre lot from his Hyde Park estate and erect with private funds a modern fireproof building to serve as a permanent repository for his papers, books, and other historical material. He set a precedent for the nation when he donated the whole—as a completed project—to the United States, to be maintained for the benefit of the public, an extensive collection of source material relating to a specific period in American history. FDR ensured even broader public interest when he provided that on his death the rest of his Hyde Park estate, including his residence, should also become the property of the United States to be used for public purposes.

The President's mother, Sara Delano Roosevelt, however,

presented a formidable obstacle to FDR's plans. Although she supported her son's lifelong penchant for collecting—indeed she had encouraged him in such pursuits since childhood—she knew that the new Library would bring the public into the private world of the family's estate even after FDR left the presidency; it threatened to permanently alter the tranquility of her beloved home, Springwood. At the very least, according to Roosevelt biographer Geoffrey Ward, she felt she had been insufficiently consulted about her son's new plans. So in the summer of 1939, she quietly boarded an ocean liner for her annual summer voyage to France without signing the deed to give the land to the government. This was not discovered until the morning of 24 July, a mere two hours before the elaborate ceremony in which FDR planned to turn over the land for the construction of the Library. After a hasty consultation with the Justice Department, FDR resolved to move forward with what was in reality little more than a charade. With the cameras rolling, the President and Mrs. Roosevelt signed the deed of gift for property to which they had no legal title. Meanwhile a copy of the deed was rushed to France and only after some cajoling did Sara finally sign the deed. The President's mother never fully reconciled herself to the Library's presence, particularly when she realized that in addition to everything else, it meant that her son would abandon his old cubbyhole of an office just off her front porch for a spacious study in the new building.[6]

President Roosevelt announced his plan for the Library at a White House press conference on 10 December 1938. Before making the plan public, he had submitted it to an advisory committee of American scholars, brought together by Harvard historian Samuel Eliot Morison. The committee was emphatically of the opinion that FDR's collections were too voluminous to be adequately preserved and administered as part of any existing library and too important for the study of recent American history to be held permanently in private custody. They smiled upon Roosevelt's plan to place the Library on his estate, recognizing the advantage of having him personally involved in the arrangement, maintenance and development of the collections. They even blessed Roosevelt's contention that Hyde Park itself was an appropriate location. With the approach of war, the President worried about the concentration of presidential papers in the Library of Congress since Washington, DC might be subject to bombing, and so suggested to the committee that Hyde Park was a particularly appropriate place for such a repository. While outside the major population centers, it was situated on what Roosevelt described—in an exaggeration duly noted by his critics— "one of the most heavily traveled roads in the country, it was in easy reach by train or automobile of the great research centers in New England, Middle Atlantic and Middle Western states."[7]

The legislation necessary to carry the President's plan into effect was passed by the 76th Congress at its first session; he signed it into law on 18 July 1939. The act placed the Library under the administration of the Archivist of the United States and authorized the Archivist to accept from Franklin D. Roosevelt "such collection of historical material" as he shall donate and to acquire by "gift, purchase or loan" other collections related to and contemporaneous with Roosevelt's own holdings. It also created a board of trustees empowered to accept and receive gifts for the Library and pledged the faith of the United States "to provide such funds as may be necessary for the upkeep of the said Library and the administrative expenses and costs of operations thereof, including the preservation and care of historical material.[8] Today's Franklin and Eleanor Roosevelt Institute is the legal successor of the original board of trustees. While it would not be formalized until 1955 with the Presidential Libraries Act, this measure marks the true beginnings of today's presidential libraries system.

Additional Collections for the Library

Always the collector, the President immediately began to seek to enlarge the Library's holdings. In remarks at the dinner with the Library's trustees on 4 February 1939, he planted the idea that the papers of New Dealers who worked with his administration belonged in the Library:

I am perfectly certain that sitting here at the table are good people, who, perhaps may not have any other disposition of their personal papers in mind, who may not wish to leave them to their own children, who may not have some particular college library to give them to. I am in great hopes that a large amount of other material will find its way to this library at Hyde Park.[9]

Later that year, and still almost two years before the Library opened, Supreme Court Justice Felix Frankfurter wrote to FDR's secretary, Missy LeHand, directing that all of his correspondence, memoranda and papers from the New Deal era be permanently deposited in the Franklin D. Roosevelt Library.[10] A grateful FDR responded to the Associate Justice, flattering him with the opinion that Frankfurter's papers "will give a far better picture of our day than mine because you, in your work, have had so much greater opportunity to analyze and suggest on paper, whereas I have been compelled to work, in great part, by word of mouth or through the medium of stodgy orders, proclamations and political speeches."[11]

FDR reached out to organizations as well as individuals. In March 1940 he wrote to Molly Dewson, head of the women's division of the Democratic National Committee:

There are in existence, so far as I know, no records of Republican or Democratic National Committees in Presidential campaigns. Automatically when a new chairman takes over the old records have been destroyed. It occurs to me that it would be a magnificent thing if the Democratic National Committee could deposit in the Library the more important of its records beginning in the year 1932.[12]

As a result, those papers were deposited in the Library. They amount to 348 linear feet and are an important research source.

The Name

Finding a name for the new institution presented something of a quandary. The new enterprise was to be a museum for the public and it was certain to be an important archive for historical researchers. Critics, of course, protested that the President was building a memorial to himself. To build the Library, FDR appointed an Executive Committee, chaired by Waldo Leland, Director of the American Council of Learned Societies. Its task was to assist him with planning the scope of the building, its equipment, the organizational needs and technical concerns about collections care and display. Officially at least, the question of the name was also left to them. Several names were proposed, discussed and rejected as not being sufficiently indicative of the Library's scope and purpose. The committee observed that in the case of other libraries that had been built around collections of former presidents—notably the Rutherford B. Hayes Memorial Library, the Hoover Institution on War, Revolution and Peace in Stanford, California (an institution distinct from the Hoover Presidential Library in West Branch, Iowa, founded in 1962) and the Harding Memorial Library—the institution became its donor's namesake. As for the choice of the word "library," the advisors and the President, not surprisingly, looked to the past for precedent as well. The word library had, for centuries, denoted the gentleman's place of study as well as the name for his collections, which often included papers and artifacts as well as books. Accordingly, the Executive Committee recommended to the President that the proposed library at Hyde Park be called the Franklin D. Roosevelt Library.[13]

Archivist R.D.W. Connor reported in a 1940 article in *American Archivist* that when the committee's recommendation was presented to him, Mr. Roosevelt earnestly demurred. He suggested instead that it should be called the "Hyde Park Library" but objection was made that this name was not sufficiently distinctive since there were six other Hyde Parks in the United States, and Hyde Park, New York already had a public library bearing that name. FDR next thought—however disingenuously—that "Crum Elbow Library" would be "swell" since Crum Elbow was part of the original tract of land from which the site of the Library would be carved. Nobody else agreed with him and the President found he was unanimously overruled by a committee entirely of his own choosing.[14]

Designing the Building

The President took a personal interest in the Library's Dutch colonial architectural design, which symbolized for him "a quality of endurance against great odds—a quality of quiet determination to conquer obstacles of nature and obstacles of man."[15] The Library was the most important of a number of Dutch colonial stone buildings built under his direction; these included his own Top Cottage, Eleanor Roosevelt's Val-Kill, Hyde Park's James Roosevelt Memorial Library, new federal post offices, and schools and libraries built throughout the Hudson Valley by Roosevelt's New Deal agencies. He loved this style because he found in it "an architecture which is good in…that it does not of necessity follow the whims of the moment but seeks an artistry that ought to be good…for all time to come. We are trying to adapt the design to the historical background of the locality and to use…the materials, which are indigenous to the locality itself. Hence the fieldstone for Dutchess County."[16]

FDR took a tremendous interest in every detail of the planning for his new Library. He worked first with Henry A. Toombs, an architect in Georgia with whom he had worked on the design of Val-kill, Top Cottage and the Little White House in Warm Springs. In 1938 Louis Simon, head architect of the General Services Administration and supervising architect of the new National Archives Building in Washington, DC, replaced Toombs. With both architects Roosevelt shared his concept of a building in the form of an open square of natural fieldstone, one story in height with a high pitched roof, built in his favored Dutch colonial style.

Insistent that ample space be made available not only for the papers but for the vast collection of naval art, ship models and gifts that he had accumulated, FDR ordered surveys of his holdings. Fred Shipman of the National Archives, who would later become the first director of the Library, assessed the archival holdings, while Laurence Vail Coleman, director of the American Association of Museums, surveyed the museum objects. Their examinations were limited to what was on hand and viewable (mostly in Washington) and did not include accurate estimates of materials located in the

Roosevelt mansion in Hyde Park, or the Roosevelt townhouse in New York, or the gubernatorial materials in Albany. Using the information gathered, Simon began work on the preliminary sketches. The external appearance of the building had already been determined by FDR and he took an active role in planning out the interior as well—the stack space, exhibit rooms, the research room and his own study.[17]

He specified separate rooms for his naval collection and a room for the use of the Dutchess County Historical Society, of which he was an early member. But neither Roosevelt nor his committee had any idea in 1938 of the vast growth that the collections were to undergo or the great crowds of visitors who were to put such a strain on the accommodations for them. They could only guess at probable increases and did not even imagine that President Roosevelt's term of office might extend beyond January 1941. Nonetheless, Roosevelt recognized early on the need for eventual expansion. He at first sketched out a series of u-shaped additions to the rear of the open square. In 1942 he made the sketches that were realized in 1969 when the Library was expanded to accommodate the Eleanor Roosevelt papers and a gallery in her honor.

The level of Roosevelt's personal involvement becomes clear from Archivist Connor's recollection of a 1939 White House meeting on the Library with the President and Waldo Leland. The three of them discussed many details down to and including what kind of containers they should use for the documents; ultimately the President specified even the design of document boxes. He also directed the exhibition of the naval art, ship models, presidential gifts, gadgets and trinkets. Leland expressed some concern that they might be allotting too much space to the museum functions of the Library. To this the President replied, "Well, you know if people have to pay a quarter to get into the Library, they will want to see something interesting inside."[18]

Not everyone was pleased with the President's determination to build a Library and museum. Mr. Clarence Boothby, a resident of Chicago, wrote to FDR on 13 December 1938:

Amid recent press reports that you plan to give your Hyde Park estate to the United States Government as a permanent memorial to yourself, provided the government and citizens will supply suitable endowment and moneys for perpetual upkeep, please accept the following humble opinion of the writer: Future generations should be allowed to forget class hatred, graft, crooked NLRB, waste, court packing, the social security fraud, communistic appointees, John Lewis, Bridges, Perkins, Earle, Guffey, Barry, Black, Murphy, Wagner, Etc., Etc.,—the TVA scandal and all the rest of your ridiculous and unworkable alphabet soup."[19]

The Library's champions outnumbered its detractors. Archibald MacLeish, Librarian of Congress—the institution that would otherwise have housed the presidential papers—spoke at the ceremony for the laying of the Library's cornerstone. He began his speech by noting that many believed that the material destined for the Roosevelt Library rightfully belonged in the Library of Congress. He then proceeded to eloquently make the case for the presidential library:

What distinguishes these papers is the fact that they are not merely the papers written in a particular sequence of years, nor the papers written by and to and about a particular man, but the papers of a Time—the papers which speak of, and speak for, and therefore recreate, a Time which the mind and the memories of man can recognize…. They belong by themselves, here in this river country, on the land in which they came.[20]

The Library Opens

The formal dedication took place on 30 June 1941, only eight days after Hitler invaded Russia. Given the gravity of the times, it was a simple ceremony with the President and his guests gathered on the flagstone walk in front of the new building. Immediately in front of them an army bugler stood, near the flagpole, accompanied by two uniformed troopers acting as the honor guard for the American flag fixed in a position to be hoisted. Newspaper reporters

FDR speaking at the dedication of the Library, June 30, 1941. FDR PRESIDENTIAL LIBRARY

and photographers stood waiting at a respectable distance.

John McShain, the Library's construction contractor, announced that the building was now complete and handed a large brass key to Frank Walker, treasurer of the corporation that had raised the money for the building from private contributions. After a few brief remarks, Walker turned the key over to Archivist Connor who accepted the building on behalf of the American people. The President closed the ceremony with a brief statement on how happy he was to see the building so well constructed and hoped it would last for many generations. FDR then raised his arm toward the flag and ordered it hoisted. As the flag was slowly raised, the assembled crowd sang "God Bless America."[21]

Library officials had no idea how many visitors to expect, but whatever the number, they would come at first only to look—not to work. Roosevelt had by then abandoned his plan to retire to a quiet life working on his collections and remained instead President of a nation destined for war. Although between three and four thousand books and some 15,000 cubic feet of records had been received at Hyde Park, the bulk of the material that would form the Library remained in Washington. In a 22 June 1941 interview for the *Hudson Valley Sunday Courier*, Library director Fred Shipman admitted, "We have nothing to excite scholars yet. We have important segments but we haven't continuous records of any one subject." He added that the staff hoped to complete the earlier files and open them to the public reasonably soon.

Reasonably soon would be 1 May 1946, thirteen months after FDR's death. It was then that the Library's Research Room was open to scholars. Roosevelt himself had favored a policy of opening the papers as soon as possible and most of his papers were available to the public in 1951. Thus only six years following the President's death, about 85 percent of FDR's presidential papers were opened for research—an event without precedent in our nation's history. The bulk of the restricted material related to foreign policy and military operations of World War II and did not become available until the early 1970s.

In the early years the museum was the public focus. The first 25-cent admission fee was collected on July 1, the day after the formal dedication. The first ticket buyer was a lifelong Republican, Floyd B. Avery of White Plains, NY. "I'm a Republican but I think it is a very interesting collection," he commented after viewing the exhibits. On its first business day the Library took in 161 admission fees, a cash total of $40.25.[22]

On that summer day spent in Hyde Park, Mr. Avery and other early museum visitors saw the President's room in the corner of the first floor, suggesting the living room of a comfortable home. The fireplace, then as now, was faced with antique Delft tiles, each carefully placed in the location according to FDR's plan. The walls were painted a subtle green-gray, the woodwork a slightly darker shade. Books were everywhere: in the secretary opposite the fireplace, in built-in bookcases in the President's study, in great piles on two tables near FDR's desk. In these early days, the President himself came and went frequently (and privately) by a door at the left of the fireplace.

The historical society's room, the Dutchess County Room, was in the southeast corner of the building. A colored map of Dutchess and Putnam counties hung on the east wall and a newspaper page of twelve scenes of Hyde Park in the late 19th century hung opposite. A rather slim collection of books on Dutchess County was housed in a cabinet on the other side of the room.

The collection in the naval exhibition room contained some 125 ship models, most of them of early sailing vessels, displayed on side and center tables. The walls, covered with oyster-white monk's cloth, were filled with paintings and colored prints of marine scenes, battles and famous vessels. In the main exhibition room, lighted cases showed presidential gifts from dignitaries and foreign heads of state. In smaller cases on either side of the main entrance were original drafts of the President's major addresses, including his speech accepting the 1932 presidential nomination; his "I hate war" speech delivered in 1936; and the "Victory Dinner" speech from 1937. Other cases contained stamp albums selected from FDR's large collection and exhibits of photographs of the Roosevelt family.

Two galleries, the "oddities" and the vehicle rooms, were located in the basement. Vehicles on display included old sleighs, carriages and two iceboats—FDR's own "Hawk" and the famous "Icicle" that won his uncle, John Roosevelt, many an iceboat racing title. With the opening just eighteen days away, FDR was busy directing the layout of exhibits as seen in this memo to Library Director Shipman: "I enclose two copies of prints enlarged from a Kodak, showing me at the helm of the ice yacht *Hawk*. I suggest that you have this framed and hung on the wall over the spars. It can be labeled 'FDR at helm of ice yacht Hawk off Roosevelt Point, 1905.'" With the memo he forwarded two photographs.[23]

Franklin D. Roosevelt Presidential Library and Museum

Officially named the "Gift Room," the things displayed in the "oddities room" were chosen from the thousands of gifts presented to the President and Mrs. Roosevelt by admirers from all over the world. Some were indeed quite odd, such as the seven-foot high papier-mâché Sphinx carrying FDR's visage, complete with cigarette holder. It was presented to him at the 1939 Washington (press corps) Gridiron Dinner when he was dodging questions about running for a third term. Many gifts represent the work of talented amateurs, while the finest designers and craftsmen made others. Nicknamed "oddities" by the President, they ran the gamut from the artistic to the homely, clever, patriotic, personal, serious, witty or broadly humorous. FDR took tremendous interest in these tokens of affection and proudly displayed them in the museum.

FDR Working in the Library

During trips home to Hyde Park, Roosevelt managed to spend as much time as he could in the Library, sorting and classifying his records and memorabilia. It was wartime then and from his study in the Library FDR delivered two of his famous "fireside chats" and two major addresses.[24] He loved to show the place to important visitors. Winston Churchill, China's Madame Chiang Kai-shek, Princess Martha of Norway, and King George of Greece—all signed the blue leather guest book FDR kept in his study.

He worked closely with Margaret Suckley, his cousin and close confidante, who was appointed a member of the Library staff in September 1941. Along with other staff she catalogued and arranged the documents, books and objects that poured in from Washington. Suckley kept a diary, which is an invaluable record of those early years, a time when the nation's business was conducted in part from FDR's Presidential Library. Most of the time Roosevelt conducted private matters there, finding respite in the minutiae of his collections, as, for example, recounted in Suckley's entry for 13 September 1943:

> The P. came Friday morning in the midst of it all—I got him a seat cushion off one of the big blue chairs and ensconced him on the floor in front of a cupboard—He worked there for an hour and a half while I flew around getting things done, my desk piled high, two trucks and a table full of things waiting to be taken care of.[25]

Or, again, in this entry from 23 May 1944:

> The President sat on the yellow covered sofa, his feet on the new stand made down in the shop…. I suggested the new Persian rug from the Shah of Persia for his room at the Library and while he was resting, we all got to work at it…. It took 10 years to make this rug and it is supposed to be worth $20,000. There are 50 knots to the square inch. It feels like velvet, has every possible color and harmonizes with everything. It is really beautiful and perfect for this particular room….[26]

On 14 April 1945 she made her final entry on FDR and his Library: "One of the hardest things I have had to do was coming [sic] to this Library on Tuesday morning, with the realization that F will never be seen here again, and that his body lies at rest in the garden." She expressed what everybody here in Hyde Park knew:

The most interesting period of this Library is over, the period of the President's association with it. What we must try to do is make it the kind of place the President wanted it to be—His spirit is here, and when I get a sort of helpless, 'what's the use in doing anything' feeling, I can feel his thought that no matter what happens, one must never give up—that was his motto and the reason of his greatness. The president's room I hope will remain as it is always—for he fixed it this way, placed the furniture, had the pictures hung, etc....[27]

It has not been difficult for subsequent Library staff to fulfill Suckley's wish because the Roosevelt presence remains forever vital. Thousands of researchers, millions of museum visitors, and hundreds of staff have worked at and visited the Franklin D. Roosevelt Presidential Library since it opened more that sixty years ago. Today the Library's education programs and website serve millions more. The collection now numbers more that 17 million pages of archival documents and audiovisual materials; the museum collection has nearly 25,000 objects. A few may take for granted the astounding collection of material gathered in this small fieldstone building and the remarkable body of research that it has generated, but none are unaffected by the force of Roosevelt's character. It is seen in the choices he made for his Library, and even more so in the spirit of reform and public service documented in the papers and artifacts housed here. With eloquence and an enduring relevance, they express the accomplishments and the energy of both Franklin and Eleanor Roosevelt.

NOTES

1. Geoffrey Ward, "Future Historians Will Curse As Well As Praise Me," *Smithsonian* (December 1989): 58.

2. Ibid.

3. FDRL, President's Personal File, FDR Library File, "Samuel Morison's remarks at a dinner on 4 February 1939 at the Hotel Carlton, Washington, DC."

4. Ward, *Smithsonian.*

5. Roosevelt, "Remarks at the Dedication of the Franklin D. Roosevelt Library at Hyde Park, New York," 30 June 1941.

6. Ward, *Smithsonian*.

7. R.D.W. Connor, "The Franklin D. Roosevelt Library," *The American Archivist* 3 (April 1940): 81-92.

8. Donald McCoy, "The Beginnings of the Franklin D. Roosevelt Library," *Prologue: Journal of the National Archives* 7 (Fall 1975): 137-150.

9. Roosevelt, "Remarks at a Dinner with the Library's Trustees," 4 February 1939.

10. FDRL, President's Personal File, FDR Library File, "Felix Frankfurter to Missy LeHand," 20 November 1939. Frankfurter's papers, however, were not deposited.

11. FDRL, President's Personal File, FDR Library File, "FDR to Frankfurter, 21 November 1939.

12. FDRL, President's Personal File, FDR Library File, "FDR Memo for Molly Dewson," 28 March 1940.

13. Connor, *The American Archivist*.

14. Connor, *The American Archivist*

15. Roosevelt, "Greeting by Telephone to the Holland Society of New York," 17 January 1935.

16. Roosevelt, "Address at the Dedication of the New Post Office in Rhinebeck, New York," 1 May 1939.

17. Waldo Leland, "The Creation of the Franklin D. Roosevelt Library: A Personal Narrative," *The American Archivist* 1 (January 1955): 11-29.

18. Leland, *The American Archivist*.

19. FDRL, President's Personal File, FDR Library File, "Clarence Boothby to FDR," 13 December 1938.

20. FDRL, President's Personal File, FDR Library File, "Remarks of Archibald Macleish," 19 November 1939.

21. FDRL, President's Personal File, FDR Library File, "Report on Groundwork of the Franklin D. Roosevelt Library by Matthew M. Epstain," 15 March 1941.

21.? FDRL, President's Personal File, FDR Library File, Newspaper clipping, *Washington Post*, 2 July 1941.

22. FDRL, President's Personal File, FDR Library File, "Presidential Memorandum for Mr. Shipman," 12 June 1941.

23. The term "fireside chat" refers to Franklin Roosevelt's informal radio broadcasts; he delivered approximately 30 fireside chats during his administration. On 7 September 1942 FDR delivered a fireside chat regarding the cost of living and the progress of the war from the Library, as well as one regarding the Cairo and Teheran Conference on 24 December 1943. In addition he delivered two major addresses—a Fourth of July address (4 July 1941) and a Labor Day address (1 September 1941)—from the Library.

24. Geoffrey Ward, *Closest Companion* (Boston: Houghton Mifflin Co., 1995), 237.

25. Ibid, 316.

26. Ibid, 423-24.

Mining and Managing History
Joyce C. Ghee

Introduction

Fans of the Indiana Jones films will recall the last scene in *Raiders of the Lost Ark,* a cavernous warehouse filled with huge, seemingly unmarked, wooden crates into which the Ark of the Covenant, encased in a similar crate, was being wheeled for storage. The implication was that no one, save Professor Jones, the intrepid fictional archeologist and adventurer, would ever be able to find it again. This greatest of all historical treasures would be safe from the hands of those who would misuse its powers, while still available to its protector when needed for the good of mankind.

Fiction is fun, but the United States had a real and equally intrepid champion of the historical search, one with that same adventurous spirit and powerful compulsion to solve history's enigmas. Franklin Delano Roosevelt, a Dutchess County product and the Nation's popular and resourceful 32nd President, might have been a model for Professor Jones. The archival storage areas and vaults

Joyce Ghee is a resident of Hyde Park, where she and her family have lived, less than a mile from the Roosevelt Estate, for almost fifty years. She is a past president of Dutchess County Historical Society. The experiences of Miss Reynolds as a founding member of DCHS and as a public historian working with FDR are particularly meaningful to the author. As Dutchess County Historian from 1981 to 1991, Mrs. Ghee found herself treading the same paths and dealing with the same problems that Reynolds and FDR contended with in preserving, historical infrastructure, and mounting major historical commemorations. The author is indebted to Eileen Hayden, DCHS Executive Director, for her assistance in editing content and providing historical perspective on Miss Reynolds' DCHS colleagues.

of the FDR Library might even look to the uninitiated like the Ark's warehouse, but they are not. Everything there (all those grey, acid-free identical boxes) is numbered, computer-indexed and accessible for easy retrieval for any verifiable and legal research project.

Had he not had so many other important matters on his plate, FDR could easily and happily have turned to solving history's mysteries as a vocation. He loved intrigue and being privy to history's little known personal secrets. There are references in correspondence with Helen Henry (who assisted him with several writing projects, ca. 1925-1926) to negotiations with *Liberty* magazine to do personal "sketches" of historical figures and to his interest in the idea of a series of film shorts presenting unexplored dramatic moments in history. He needed no fictional adventurer's ammunition when he could call for assistance upon friends, family, personal charm, an adequate bank account, political debtors and the power of the political positions he held during his adult lifetime. He had no difficulty using all such resources to satisfy an insatiable need to know and to collect, combined with the incredible self-confidence that encouraged him in every case to trust in his own judgment. Solving history's conundrums provided him momentary escape from the pressures of work or office. Following his struggle with polio it was something pleasurable to look forward to. Discovering, collecting and displaying his historical "finds" was his "play," and unlike Indiana Jones' storehouse FDR's gatherings are accessible.

Public weal and the American people are the beneficiaries of FDR's need to discover history and to put it to his own purposes. The results of his passion for history are incalculable, impacting virtually every state in the union. He reintroduced Americans to their own local history, culture, art, and architecture through government surveys and projects that put people to work. Using these resources thematically, he reinforced our sense of place and our spirit as a people. We are fortunate that he used his toolbox so wisely. More than sixty years after his death, his sense of the value of history still enriches us in countless ways: the nation's first presidential library, the identification and preservation of important historic sites and structures, the erection of public edifices that reflect their territories, the lasting results of art and architectural enterprises, historic document surveys, writers' and historians' projects, and environmental programs inspired by and emerging from local knowledge of an area. Recapturing the history and culture of communities across the face of the country began right here in Dutchess County with FDR-initiated searches, projects and experiments.

Forging a Manager and Miner of History

Those who work with the many users of history will readily agree that "everyone loves history," hearing its tales, enjoying its celebrations. Some love reading and exploring the more serious history. FDR's serious work with history gave him great pleasure.

Knowledge of history provides explanations for the choices made and courses taken by individuals and communities, pouring light upon the present or on a particular situation. Hardly anyone realizes, until they have to do it, how difficult it can be to do historical research and the importance of original sources. One needs the document, the proof, the evidence. Finding, identifying and verifying the evidence are the marks of a confident, serious historian.

The making of an interested and confident authority, such as FDR proved to be, is essential in understanding his ultimate contributions to the field. He would, no doubt, have made a fine academic historian had he not been both a congenital manager of outcomes and a born politician who enjoyed politics and the limelight. Those characteristics took precedence over scholarly urges. His interest in causal relationships and in knowing more than others may have emerged in part from his upbringing in a family consumed with its own past, a very interesting group whose carefully kept, first-hand histories most certainly impacted him personally. He had a position and role to fill, laid out by ancestors and ratified by immediate family. Nonetheless, it would seem that, despite the need for acclaim and family approval (and his own craving to rise higher in public life than had any other family member), he clung to the vision of himself in the role of historian in the retirement he planned but never lived to see. He wanted to have both. Like the Sinatra song, "I Did It My Way," FDR did history *"his* (sic) way."

He used his understanding of history differently than conventional historians. He turned an all-consuming avocation— collecting—into a creative tool to reconstruct American society. To do this he built upon a foundation of personal knowledge of history fostered by a family who believed that *its* history was significant. He forged an ingrained acquisitive bent to collect in numerous categories (stamps, birds, documents, books, naval and political ephemera, etc.), encouraged by his parents as an educational tool, into the foundation of his history management style. Using the power of his personal charm and social/political positions, he learned to surround himself with professionals who knew how to do specific tasks related to collecting, preserving, and applying the lessons of history. His *modus operandi* was to engage others as partners in the search or the task. Today's managers might call it "team building." The evidence is clear that most of those called upon for service were happy to provide it and, indeed, felt honored. Margaret "Daisy" Suckley and Helen Wilkinson Reynolds, two Dutchess County women, perhaps bore the local burden of that honor more than others. Their reward was to be a part of his accomplishment.

The vocations essential to collecting, caring for, and making the many guises of history accessible are legion. They include many specialists, among them academics, local and municipal historians, genealogists, folklorists, archivists, archaeologists, antiquarians and purveyors/dealers of documents and antiques, conservators, curators of material culture, and the museum administrators who have managerial responsibilities for historical institutions, museums, sites, archives and departments of government. Their work provides the bits and pieces of our history, which interpreters, writers and educators pull together in meaningful ways for the rest of us. Early on, FDR came to understand the importance of each role and brought the best practitioners into his circle.

Helen Wilkinson Reynolds, circa 1915, around the time she and others founded
the Dutchess Country Historical Society.
ADRIANCE MEMORIAL LIBRARY, LOCAL HISTORY COLLECTION

His plans for the nation's first Presidential Library germinated in his mind for a number of years before they were laid out for public scrutiny in 1938/39. By that time he had already identified individuals whose work was known to him and with whom he had worked to be part of the planning process or support staff.

Miss Reynolds was one of the finest researchers and writers of history produced in this area. FDR recognized her talent early. She had curatorial, bibliographic and archival skills gleaned from years of advocacy for better care of municipal and historic documents and from working within area educational and cultural institutions, caring for and using collections. She had also served as a government historian for both Dutchess County and the City of Poughkeepsie. Although not part of the kinship of the "River Families," she could claim an eastern Dutchess County genealogy with ties to the wealthy Carys and Flaglers, families as distinguished and long-standing as any of the county's earliest settlers. Reynolds/ Wilkinson family businesses along the river had made commercial history. FDR's long-term business relationship with her was also a warm friendship based upon "quid pro quo." She helped him and he helped her. He saw Miss Reynolds as *the* authority on Hudson Valley history and envisioned her as director/ curator of local and regional collections destined for the Dutchess Room in his library.

Margaret "Daisy" Suckley was a distant cousin and descendent, like FDR, of the Beekmans, one of the oldest land holding clans in the valley. She shared the common River Families historic legacy (the knowledge of personal histories), had access to the homes they inhabited and institutions they had created, and had earned FDR's trust by being a willing and faithful confidante of his shared secrets. As the only wage earner in a family living proudly just above genteel poverty in the family manse, "Wilderstein" in Rhinebeck, she also was in need of employment. He looked to her to assist him with the care of his private files and groomed her for a role in his retirement as a confidential assistant and archivist for personal family papers at the library he planned. Suckley's story and the unfolding of FDR's plans for her role as his aide during the retirement years are clearly told by Geoffrey C. Ward in his book *Closest Companion,* based upon her diary notations and personal correspondence with the President.

FDR selected for himself the role of projects manager—*the* manager among managers of history, because he was also one of the best miners of history. Nowhere is his managerial style more evident than in Dutchess County where his collections and institutional impacts are closely gathered together and the record of those who participated in his many history projects is more easily discovered.

The history of Hyde Park and Dutchess County was *his* story. This place became his laboratory for experiments applied to the wider fields to come. Hometown and home county represent the microcosm that became a New Deal macrocosm. Childhood training reinforced by a loving home environment and generous parental approval of his familial history successes produced the self-confidence needed for his independent dual adult roles of miner and manager. His youthful successes here were the model for greater productions on state and national stages. But the valley and this county were not just his laboratory, they were a part of the earth that he dearly loved, the place he brought friends, political colleagues, royalty and world leaders, whenever he wanted to charm them, relax them and impress them.

Many historians and authors have documented FDR's family genealogy. The first Roosevelt to step off the boat from the Netherlands, mid 1600s, was Nicholas Martensen van Roosevelt who died in 1659, a resident of Manhattan. The first Isaac Roosevelt,[1] whose Revolutionary War service was repaid in land and who made his descendants proud by voting for New York's ratification of the U.S. Constitution in 1788, was the first family member to claim land in Dutchess. FDR's father, James, (named for his grandfather) moved from Poughkeepsie to Hyde Park during his first marriage after the family home, Mount Hope, was lost to fire. FDR's father was a highly successful businessman and railroad executive who established the family's country seat at Springwood, on the "flatts"—a rich farmland plateau along the riverbank south of the Hyde Park hamlet.

Such highlights of family history are the tip of the iceberg. Knowledge of every Roosevelt, male and female, and every degree of relationship among them, was ingrained. As a member of the River Families society, such genealogical ephemera and personal connections to the record of the past in America and the world were the foundation of a history curriculum taught by word, example, and tutors cognizant of the importance of such information. Home schooling with the Rogers children in Hyde Park and frequent travel abroad led FDR eventually to Groton and Harvard. At every step he would be surrounded by family influence and indirect tutelage in the form of visits and tête-à-têtes with immediate and distant members of family, relatives, old schoolmates, teachers, business associates or members of their social set. His mother, "Mr. James'" second wife, Sara Delano Roosevelt, was his primary tutor. She taught her son the importance of family history and made it the doorway to knowledge of world history, of which her own father, Warren Delano, and his business ventures in the Orient were an exciting part.

The value that both his parents placed on their family history as influential to the course of world history, from the time of the patentees, Henry Beekman and Robert Livingston, to distant cousin President Theodore Roosevelt, is evidenced by their hoarding tendencies. Roosevelts saved everything: papers, letters, photos, books, documents, furniture, clothing, paintings, crockery, toys, tools, memorabilia, and odds and ends of all kinds that were part of a personal story that has become part of our collective history. What was once managed by the Roosevelt family is now managed by The National Park Service and the FDR Library, primarily because FDR was such a zealous miner of history whose wise management included a secure plan for the future care of his collections and properties. He purposely intended that the materials, which he knew had value, would become a national resource. Historian Geoffrey C. Ward calls FDR "a self-confessed pack-rat" who admitted that he was "a mine for which future historians will curse…as well as praise me."[2]

Techniques of Mining History in Dutchess County

Exploring the "mine" and learning how to manage it began at home with FDR where the "mother lode" was first uncovered, but spread in manhood throughout all of Dutchess County and the Hudson Valley. The story of FDR's first serious attempt to research and write history as an undergraduate student at Harvard is told by Ward and other historians. Franklin's attention to capturing history began with the pivotal documentation of his family history, "The Roosevelts of New Amsterdam" as a thesis for a History 10 course.[3] It was heavily dependent upon Sara Roosevelt's personal family knowledge and well-kept collection of genealogical source materials. By proving the authenticity of his early Dutch roots in the founders of New Amsterdam and his historic connections to the Netherlands, his work on that history paper helped him to be elected to membership in the Holland Society in 1910 and secured him a trusted place among its elite leadership. The usefulness of being a member of that prestigious body during the period of his run for state senate certainly lends credence to claims that acquiring knowledge of history is a practical skill.

FDR's speechwriting style always brilliantly captured the essence of an idea and sold it, either in the writing or in the editing and delivery. His imprint on written local history, however, is less in what he wrote about it than in his interest and support of research and special projects. The local history articles and materials on which he put his name often were the result of work for hire or in return for a favor by another who did the research or transcribed an original hand-written document with which Roosevelt was familiar, an accepted academic approach. His contributions, in part because of the time restraints of other duties, were often brief introductions providing an historic context for original sources, e.g. the documents and records of the Town of Hyde Park. He enjoyed doing the initial research to know that the topic was important and that the documentation was available; that was the miner in him. After his struggle with polio, the wide personal search would have been severely limited had his determination and innate management skills not taken over. From the mid-1920s the cadre of trained local miners at his disposal (his history team) would be given its assignments.

Where did all of those willing volunteers come from? During FDR's youth and young manhood there was no local historical society, either in Hyde Park, or in Dutchess. There were, however, other venues besides family and one's social set in which to find those knowledgeable about the past. There was also the opportunity to help build an historical society.

After his father's death in 1900, young Franklin was destined to be the head of the family. His father, James, an important local civic leader, had held a number of positions in the community: as member of the local school board, a St. James Vestryman and the Hyde Park Town Supervisor, among other offices. It was expected that his son would also show interest in such public service. Franklin, too, would be involved in the community as a member of St. James Vestry, the fire company and Grange. These, added to involvement in other county organizations, political groups, and community activities gave him access to a new and different constituency of informal tutors outside the family social circle, the people who lived and worked in the area: farmers, small business owners, housewives, church leaders, and elected officials of the town and county. Older residents of the area appreciated his unfeigned interest in their personal recollections of community life in the past. Political associations with Judges John Mack and Joseph Morschauser opened many doors for him. Roosevelt historians are familiar with the names of many of these acquaintances. Men like Benjamin Haviland and Moses Smith, although not "River Family" gentility, happily shared their knowledge, local gossip, folklore or experiential wisdom. He learned much from them and they enjoyed basking in either the light of his interest or his successes. They also became his constituents when he ran for office, beginning with the run for a New York State Senate seat in 1910. They remained his allies over the years as he turned the information and materials he had gathered, with their help, into tools for developing not only his own career but also community institutions such as libraries, schools, public buildings and programs.

Forming and Mining a County Historical Society

The lack of a county historical society was addressed in the spring of 1914 when a small group of local men and women met in the Pleasant Valley Library. Their concern was that the history of the area was in jeopardy because there was no institution created to collect, care for and make such history accessible. At a second meeting on May 26th working by-laws for a local historical society were presented. A motion by Poughkeepsie physician, Dr. John W. Poucher, to name it the Dutchess County Historical Society was passed unanimously.[4] Over the course of that year committees met to draft a mission statement and constitution and to plan activities and lectures. At each reporting meeting more interested persons had applied for membership and by the close of the year there were more than 150 members. The Hon. Franklin D. Roosevelt, Assistant Secretary of the Navy at the time, who sensed the society's significance, was among those charter members.

A number of serious professionals and respected local historians were among the charter members. State Senator Edmund Platt, former journalist and historian, James Baldwin, Ph.D. of Vassar College faculty, Dr. Poucher, Miss Reynolds, and Attorney John J. Mylod represented the best among Poughkeepsie's history seekers and keepers. By the end of the following year, FDR's mother and half brother were also listed in the Year Book as members, as were descendants of Hyde Park's first settlers, the Stoutenburghs, and others with ties of friendship or family to the Roosevelts: Dows, Delanos, and Suckleys. FDR's neighbors, the Hon. Thomas Newbold of Hyde Park and George S. Van Vliet, respected local historian and document collector of Staatsburg, were included among the elected town vice presidents of the Society along with the noted Columbia University scholar and social theoretician Prof. Joel E. Spingarn of Amenia.[5] It was a stellar hive of both worker bees and potential

Meeting of the Dutchess County Historical Society at FDR's home: (*l* to *r*) John A. Mylod, Helen Wilkinson Reynolds, W. Platt Adams, President of the Society, FDR, and Eleanor Roosevelt. FDR PRESIDENTIAL LIBRARY

queen bees whose mission was sympathetic to FDR's purposes.

The earliest mission of the Society as stated in its bylaws of 1914 was three-fold:

> 1–to collect the history of New York State as it particularly dealt with Dutchess County, (in the broadest terms, this included natural, civil, literary, and ecclesiastical history);
> 2–to encourage historical research, writing of papers and delivery of lectures;
> 3–to collect, display, and care for objects of historical interest.[6]

Society leaders immediately began to work on all three initiatives. With the endorsement of serious historians, the membership of representatives of the area's oldest resident families and the blessings of members of the River Families, Dutchess County Historical

Society (DCHS) rose quickly in stature and influence. Roosevelt found in its gatherings and in its publications the core of recruits, information on sources, and inspiration for many history projects to come.

DCHS gathered together many talented, collegial "miners," open to ideas and eager to get started. Their numbers and skills continued to swell, bolstered by FDR's interest, his rising fortunes and their own enthusiasms.

DCHS and FDR—A Case Study—Developing a History Partnership

Franklin D. Roosevelt was an involved and active member of DCHS who assisted at times behind the scenes, and at times publicly. He was a member from 1914 until his death, and served as a Vice President for the Town of Hyde Park from 1926 to 1945, through his terms as Governor of New York State and as President of the United States. During this entire period he was personally engaged in Society affairs as: a supporter of and investor in the research and publication projects undertaken by others, a DCHS ambassador, a provider of entree, a generous donor, and a genial host to the Society and to its individual members. FDR was also a contractor of specifically talented, proven history workers. These he engaged for his own pet projects as well as for the work of the Society.

While Society collecting, initially, was done broadly, its focus from the onset was locating source documents, also a favorite FDR pursuit. Helen Reynolds shared this interest. Her public research and writing career began with the self-publishing of her seminal history of Christ Church in 1911 based upon her research in church records. She had been an influential, active, working member of the Society from its beginning. Her impact on the Year Book series, as an early contributor and later as co-editor with Henry Booth, is evident a few years after the earliest editions. From 1922, when she became Year Book editor, until her death in 1943 she *was* the Year Book. It reflected her policies, her research and her insistence that documenting history with original sources was DCHS's most important task. Although lacking the degrees marking an academic, she was in truth a natural scholar, for whom academia was a magnet. Friendships over the years with Vassar faculty and administration: historian Lucy Maynard Salmon, folklorist Constance Varney Ring, botanist Edith A. Roberts, President Henry MacCracken, and others allowed her access to ideas, facilities, and contacts far beyond what might be expected of a "local historian." Miss Salmon's unique approach as an educator to the study of history, using original sources to teach college undergraduates, was the approach favored by Reynolds and also Roosevelt.

Roosevelt and Reynolds had much in common. Both shared the sense of adventure of uncovering new history and a dogged determination to finish what they had started. Both were dedicated Episcopalians and members of old Dutchess County families. Reynolds, suffering from a spinal affliction from childhood, shared with FDR the agony of pain and the frustration of disability. Her work was known and respected by FDR and he saw in her a collaborator and supporter. Their most extensive publishing partnership was the production under the sponsorship of the Holland Society of Miss Reynolds' book on Dutch houses in the Hudson Valley, an idea emerging from FDR's love of Dutch vernacular architecture and his concern for its loss. Discussions from 1923 with Holland Society Secretary, Frederick J. Keator, resulted at length in a formal proposal from FDR to the Trustees of the Holland Society, outlined in a September 30, 1924 letter now in the President's correspondence files of the Franklin D. Roosevelt Library. It foresaw a publication project of three volumes done by separate authors. Helen Henry was to handle Long Island, New York City and New Jersey. Helen Wilkinson Reynolds would handle the Hudson Valley. FDR, as chair of a Holland Society Committee on Preserving Dutch Houses, would manage details of the publishing and fund-raising. Dr. Poucher, also a Holland Society member, was part of the committee and stood in FDR's stead during his absences. It was an enormous task, which FDR optimistically assumed could be completed by 1925; however, it took more than five years. Miss

Reynolds did her part—the research, writing, editing and work with the project photographer. An associate of Miss Reynolds, Margaret De Mott Brown, was recommended by her for this task. Her exquisite photos would grace this book and a number of others in the future for DCHS. FDR did his part in handling the fund-raising and financial details, getting the authors what they needed by way of entree and negotiating the murky waters of major publishing houses and the old institutions of the Holland Society. Helen Henry's ill health forced her to leave her portion of the project unfinished. The completed work, *Dutch Houses in the Hudson Valley Before 1776*, considered a classic reference, has had a long and successful life. It was reprinted in recent years and it is still available after more than seventy years.

Those involved in this project continued to work together. The 1924 Year Book carries a reference to an offer made to the DCHS Trustees by FDR, Miss Reynolds and Dr. Poucher, jointly, to underwrite the publication of their works as "Occasional Publications" of the Society.[7] They included Miss Reynolds' *Poughkeepsie, the Origin and Meaning of the Word,* Dr. Poucher's and Miss Reynolds' *Old Gravestones of Dutchess County,* apparently in the process of being printed, and the Hon. F.D. Roosevelt's *Records of the Town of Hyde Park*, a work in progress. In a letter written to FDR by Miss Reynolds on September 24, 1924 for the purpose of developing a budget for the book on Dutch houses, she writes:

> "Then, as to my own time and labor… In the case of the Hyde Park town-books, it took me all of my daily "working" capacity for about three months, an average of one and a half to two hours at a time, in other words some one hundred hours of close work, The only way that I can think of to estimate the cost of that work would be to enquire what the rate is at Vassar for tutoring, per hour. Would that meet with your approval?" [8]

This would seem to indicate that she had assisted in the research for FDR's *Records of the Town of Hyde Park*. He had the overview, wrote the preface and the introductions to each subdivision of the collection. Reynolds served as editor for every "Occasional Publication," from concept through placing the final proof in the hands of a printer. FDR's hefty volume of town municipal and institutional records was finally published by DCHS in 1928 as Volume III in the series.[9]

He repeated the arrangement with DCHS Board, paying for the printing in the publication of *Records of Crum Elbow Precinct*, published in 1940 as Volume VII of DCHS's "Occasional Publications." He edited these documents as well and trusted that he would be repaid in the long run out of sales. A notation in the Treasurer's Annual Report of 1942 shows a credit of $10 for this book to "President Roosevelt's account." The account was in the care of Assistant Secretary Amy Pearce Ver Nooy, who assisted Miss Reynolds' work and later inherited her mantle. Both partners kept careful records.[10]

Roosevelt's contributions to the written history of the area through DCHS were many and varied. In 1923, Editor Reynolds included a brief summary by FDR of a manuscript document, which he had procured at auction in 1922: "The Minutes of the Council of Appointment of New York State- A Recovered Record of the Revolution."This brief article outlines the appointments at meetings in Poughkeepsie 1778/79 of Revolutionary leaders like George Clinton, John Jay, and Melanchthon Smith (who brokered New York's Ratification of the United States Constitution) that redefined their emerging power. FDR's role as author, collector, and donor is described in the introduction of the work as that of "an interested member" of the Society.[11] This was precisely the kind of activity that he enjoyed and would continue to enjoy for more than two decades as an active member. At the semi-annual meeting of the Society that year, he was appointed to DCHS's membership committee, along with John J. Mylod, Helen Reynolds and several others,[12] taking an even more "hands-on" role with his partners.

In 1925 Roosevelt was tapped by Governor Al Smith of New York to chair the Taconic State Parkway Commission. His long-established habit of wandering the county's back roads to find wonderful views was turned to planning a recreational highway of gentle curves, carefully planted landscapes, and stone overpasses, through the historic patent area farmlands he so loved, to open these vistas to weekenders. He called the parkway, modeled on European historic roads, "my invention."[13] It benefited from his wanderings, knowledge of local history, awareness of the work habits of local farmers and their need for safe crossings, and from his personal friendships with men like Judge John Mack, who lived in the areas which the road would traverse and who could ease the process of working with local communities.[14]

As FDR's New York State political career heated up there would be less time for membership activities, but he would find new venues in the future for his applications of local history in wide-ranging state and national public works projects. Hudson Valley projects in which he took special interest often engendered a personal response. Such was the case with DCHS publications.

Despite the press of politics and law practice he found time for another article. The 1925 Year Book included a brief paper (pp.25-28) listed with "Contributions from Members" based upon another original manuscript he had uncovered. It listed, with particulars, all of the "Vessels Employed in Public Service at Fishkill Landing October 7, 1781, John Palmer, Harbour Master."

The 1926 Year Book, on page 20, contains a Currier and Ives print acquired by Roosevelt, entitled "View of Dutchess," which appears to have stumped FDR and the whole team. A note by Reynolds along with the image asks, "Where is it?" The answer lies undetermined, but it may be in one of the thousands of pieces of correspondence he saved in the FDR Library.

Reynolds & Co.—FDR / HWR's Choices
 Shape a Project Team

In the Reynolds-FDR letters from 1923 to her death in 1943 there are many references to items that interested both of them, along with suggested strategies for acquisition. Her own limited circumstances had been made very clear to Roosevelt as they negotiated her work on the Holland Society book. Not unlike the Suckleys, she and her mother lived modestly on carefully invested funds from the family estate and on Helen's earnings from her work as an historian. She was not a collector or a vendor, but took pleasure in seeing important historical materials placed in the proper hands. She knew the system and the protocols and was sensitive to buyers' and sellers' positions. She was frequently asked to serve as his intermediary in negotiations with a potential donor or seller. Upon occasion, such items, as the Civil War draft wheel, ended as donations to the DCHS collection. More often, those that interested FDR or had a direct connection to his personal history remained in Roosevelt hands, eventually to become part of the collections of the Presidential Library where both Reynolds and Roosevelt felt they would find better care.

Miss Reynolds made no secret of her view that DCHS should focus primarily on publishing, rather than collecting. Her own experience early on with mishandled documents in the custody of local government made her a staunch advocate for high standards of museum and archival care. DCHS, operated by volunteers and contract staff, shared space in Vassar Institute and at Adriance Memorial Library for many years where she could be assured of physical protection and proper accessibility for prized documents. DCHS had no permanent home for all its collections save Poughkeepsie's modest Glebe House. It was the home of the Reverend John Beardsley, the Tory Minister of Christ Church during the American Revolution, which the Society worked to save in the late 1920s with FDR's help and encouragement. The Glebe, however, was ill-suited for an archive. During the late 1970s, long after the leadership of Reynolds and Roosevelt, DCHS found another site to house its administration and the bulk of its growing collections when it procured a long-term lease on Governor Clinton House in Poughkeepsie from New York State. The solutions that Reynolds and FDR espoused during their era were by far the best of limited choices.

Their correspondence shows a growing respect for each other's personal talents and gifts and moves from a very business-like, formal relationship, to a close respectful friendship, where favors could be asked and given and where personal feelings regarding health and the burdens of work could be easily expressed. She and those she brought into her working circle became welcome guests not only of FDR but of his family as well.

In the fall of 1927 (a year before his run for the governorship), FDR offered his home, "Springwood," as the site of the Society's annual Pilgrimage. He was a member of the planning committee and he, wife Eleanor, and his mother welcomed DCHS "pilgrims" to a tour and a talk by him on the "Water Lots" of the Nine Partners Patent followed by a picnic on the lawn, with dessert provided by the Roosevelts. Chairman for the event was John J. Mylod. He wisely allowed Miss Reynolds and Mr. Roosevelt to manage the details of organizing the transport, feeding and scheduling of the movements of an estimated 175-300 guests (dependent upon who did the count and when) around the property. It was done without making themselves unwelcome. The delighted crowd willingly followed orders and moved by foot or motorcade, as instructed "by whistle assembly," to each step of the carefully orchestrated day-long tour that finally ended at Oakleigh Thorne's Briarcliff Farms property in Pine Plains. FDR's enjoyment of sharing his knowledge of local history and of having an enthusiastic audience is nowhere more apparent than in this episode as host to his Dutchess County friends and neighbors. A photographic spread by World-Wide Photos made available to DCHS for reproduction in its 1927 Year Book shows Eleanor Roosevelt serving cookies to Mr. Mylod, a view of DCHS picnickers on the hillside, another of the crowd listening to FDR's talk, and a group close up of Roosevelt with his key history partners: Mylod and Reynolds.[15]

That same Year Book includes the page 15 announcement by Mr. Mylod at the Society's semi-annual meeting at the Nelson House of the appointment of Miss Reynolds to the position of Dutchess County Historian by the Board of Supervisors on October 21, 1927. Mr. Mylod, actively involved in local politics, openly supported Miss Reynolds' ethical stance on the issue of the county's poor care of government documents and saw the importance of government involvement in community historical celebrations. The two had been involved citizens as DCHS volunteers in a number of public advocacy efforts: historic preservation issues, government record keeping, school curriculum and historical commemorations. DCHS Minutes in the 1923 Year Book (pages15-17) reveal the interest in such issues and an example of the passion of Society advocacy in a board resolution deploring actions of legislators attempting to legislate the content of history curriculum in schools based upon "ignorance and malice." It called upon elected officials to keep personal politics out of history and leave history to historians and teaching to teachers. Reynolds' appointment to a government position of influence and honor gave Mylod great satisfaction and presented new opportunities for action. Secretary Poucher's account of that meeting shows DCHS organizational growth as an important part of a statewide history network, sharing resources, information and access to political power. Speakers at that meeting included not only General John Ross Delafield (the Livingston descendent in residence at the family Country Seat, "Montgomery Place"), but both the Hon. Edmund Platt (who by then was Vice-Governor of the Federal Reserve Board) and FDR's nemesis, the Hon. Hamilton Fish Jr., who spoke of the importance of the Hudson River during the American Revolution.

Page 24 of the 1927 Year Book introduces a copy of an 18th century Quit-Rent Lease owned by FDR and at that time "on loan" by him to the historical society in their collections repository at Vassar Institute. On the cusp of his entry into the highest offices of this nation, Roosevelt continued to be generous to those who shared his loving obsession with local history. Such documents were treasures to him, and placing them in the hands of the Society is evidence of the trust that had grown between him and his associates among Society members.

Taking on gubernatorial duties after the 1928 election in New York was no obstacle to FDR's continuing interest in local history. He would continue to support the issues his Dutchess County friends thought important such as protecting historic mile markers along major roads, a project DCHS had espoused from its inception—as evidenced by President Magill's address in the 1916-18 Year Book. Having the governor as a friend proved to be particularly useful to Reynolds. Her warm correspondence with New York State Historian, Dr. Alexander C. Flick, and State Archivist A.J.F. Van Laer in DCHS collections shows their eagerness to point her to source materials for her research on DCHS publications or to assist in accurately translating 18th century Dutch. FDR's helpful communication with his friends at DCHS continued through his two terms as governor and throughout his occupancy of the Oval Office in Washington, D.C.

As the trust in working relationships had grown, so had friendly favors. A letter from Miss Reynolds to Roosevelt in 1929 shows both of them being helpful with the other's personal research. He had loaned her a "little book about Poughkeepsie" which she would be returning to his "dear mother" in Hyde Park for her to keep until her son returned to the area. Reynolds now did him a favor in return.

> Meanwhile I have been trying to find out something of the history of your brother's place (the home of his half brother, James Roosevelt, "Rosy" Roosevelt, next-door to Springwood). As soon as I saw the foliated doorframes I thought the house was of the approximate date of "1830" and examined the deeds at the court house to learn who owned it then. As Edward and Joseph Giraud had the place 1830-1835 I made enquiry of Miss Lucy Giraud of Poughkeepsie, as granddaughter of Edward."

The letter outlines a full study of the property, with an account of information she had received from George S. Van Vliet, another trusted helper, and includes her hand-drawn maps and what she envisioned as the possible original plans of the house.[16]

The Society's pride in their member/Vice-President and their easy access to him is evident in the 1931 Year Book in an article by Miss Reynolds, "Dutchess County Gives the State a Governor" (pages 58-69). The full genealogy of the Roosevelt Hyde Park branch is accompanied by Margaret De Mott Brown's portrait of FDR, re-done photographs of a drawing of Mount Hope and an old photo of Springwood prior to FDR's redesign in 1914 to compare with a recent photo (1931) of the home. Miss Reynolds sent the article with a cover letter on October 3, 1931 to the governor for his approval and editing. She hated intruding on what must have been a brief vacation for FDR but needed his edits as soon as possible for a proof that had to be completed by mid-October. His response to her, sent October 13th, indicates that he thought it was a fine paper and also that he respected her deadline. However, he appended fourteen suggested edits to improve, correct or question information. He thought that it most important for her to state that Isaac Roosevelt, his great-great grandfather, was not merely a delegate to New York's Ratification Convention of 1788 but was from the outset *in favor* of ratification. Her sensitive editing pleased him.[17] A *New York Times* article October 1, 1933, "Roosevelt's Dutchess County Connection Dates From 1752," credited Reynolds' 1932 DCHS Year Book paper as their source for the data.[18]

There was more of the same to come as FDR won the election to become President of the United States at one of the lowest points in our nation's history. Reynolds expressed the feelings of not only DCHS members and leaders, but of many of her fellow citizens in a letter to the outgoing governor dated November 13, 1932.

> How is a friend and neighbor who voted for you to tell you the things that surge up in her mind and heart? On the flyleaf of a book you once gave me you called me your fellow-worker in the field of history and I valued that designation for several reasons. As I wrote you last June when you were nominated for the Presidency, you are *making* history and I, who love to *record it,* look on eagerly, both as a friend and historian....But how am I to express my pride that a son of our beloved Dutchess is to be head of the nation?....Now, again, as last June I would say that

the greatest wish I can offer you is that in 'making history,' you may be known by the generations that come after as a President who, in troubled days wrought helpfully for a confused and suffering humanity."

Her emotional letter ends, interestingly enough, with a request for her and Dr. Poucher to see him in Hyde Park in order to talk to him about his "Broadside about Hyde Park"—a short article for the 1932 Year Book. His eagerness to confer with them at this crucial moment in his life about a short history paper is quite evident. Considering all that faced him in closing down a state administration and preparing for his new responsibilities, his response came quickly with a "thank you" for the nice note and an immediate "yes" for Reynolds and Dr. Poucher to visit. He wanted them to call when he arrived early in December.[19]

The Broadside in question was an advertisement from John Bard in 1768 marketing land in Hyde Park to residents of New York. It was printed in the 1932 Year Book (pages 80-82) with a brief introduction by Reynolds noting that as the publication went to press FDR was being elected president. The document was preceded by a brief introductory history by the contributor—FDR.

The relationships with Dutchess County Historical Society members, strengthened by commonly held interests and values and jointly undertaken projects during the years prior to his presidency, became fast friendships during the difficult years all concerned faced during the Great Depression and World War II. Probably one of the best proofs of this is a hand-written letter to the President by Reynolds on April 1, 1933.

"Dear Mr. President
Can you, Oh! Can you, help the holders of guaranteed mortgages in New York!
My agony of mind is so great I must cry out to you! Apparently our guarantee is gone. We don't know whether we have anything to count on.
Mother is 82—I could not leave her to go to work if work were to be had. This seems to mean annihilation.... Only a desire

*to keep faith in God, not to lose ideals, keeps me from utter
despair.
And your example in your illness of courage + (sic) will to win
is an inspiration to me!
Oh, haste with Federal aid to New York.*
   Yours
   Helen Reynolds"[20]

Yet, with all of the burdens he faced, he read her letter and responded in a way that would calm her fears. The President's reply was, for the first time in a correspondence of some years length, to "Dear Helen"—not Miss Reynolds—and it came speedily on April 5th. This was the reply of a caring friend who, although under great stress himself and the recipient of thousands of similar messages, took the time to frame the response himself and to share with her the thinking of those who were helping him build a strategy for financial recovery.

> Dear Helen:
>
> I am working hard to accomplish something in the New York City mortgage situation, although the Federal government can do little more than reorganize the mortgage companies into some kind of general pool. This undoubtedly means cutting the interest rate but, at the same time, they tell me that most, if not all, of the principal will be saved.
>
> I realize fully what a hardship it is. There may be a little delay, of course, but it simply has to be worked out somehow.
> Always sincerely, *FDR* [21]

One might consider that this exchange took place within a month of his inauguration, shortly after an assassin's attempt on his life, at a time when he was forming his administration, closing and opening banks, testing the gold standard in world markets, weighing federal strategies to control the stock market and securities and initiating public works programs, e.g., the Civilian Conservation Corps.[22] The problems of the nation weighed heavily on him and the advisors who surrounded him, yet the correspondence and interactions with DCHS and its members, primarily through Helen Reynolds, continued, not as a distraction, but as a source of comfort and pleasure.

Teamwork Produces Results

His words obviously gave Reynolds the courage to cope with even more reduced financial circumstances than she and her mother had already faced. But another request from FDR at the end of April directed her attention to *his* "needs." He wanted her to do some research on the source of "Kromme Elleboog" (Crum Elbow). The territory to which this original Dutch place name applied was a *very* personal irritation to him. He was convinced that it belonged to Hyde Park. An Ulster County property owner across the Hudson thought otherwise. Reynolds' research in Dutchess County records and historical materials took her mind off guaranteed mortgages and proved helpful to FDR who eventually had the name placed securely on official government maps, precisely where he thought it belonged. Reynolds' investigation of the subject appeared as a meticulously researched article in the 1933 Year Book. She gives credit to all those who assisted her: New York State Archivist A.J.F. Van Laer, Edna Jacobsen of the New York State Library Manuscripts and History Section, Dorothy Barck of the New York Historical Society staff, Reginald Pelham Bolton of the Museum of the American Indian, Heye Foundation staff, Clarence Elting of Highland and two DCHS members, historian George S. Van Vliet and Attorney Henry Hackett, FDR's family lawyer. With such an array of support Roosevelt had no doubt that he was right in claiming Kromme Elleboog for his Hyde Park home.[23]

That same Year Book included Reynolds' report on the celebration of the County's 250th anniversary, which included a well-wisher's message from the president (page23). More historically significant was his brief account in an open letter to Miss Reynolds of the background of his first radio address to the American public on March 5, 1933 when all banks were closed—the first of the famous "Fireside Chats." It was an inspired use of a new media and a *modus operandi* that made every citizen—those as worried as Reynolds had been—aware of what their government and their president were doing to deal with serious problems affecting them all. In explaining why he chose to make the delivery so simple and straightforward, in part, he wrote:

> ...I asked three or four gentlemen...to let me have... their thoughts on what I should say in a public radio statement.... I read the suggestions, discussed them informally with...friends and came to the conclusion that the imperative purpose would not be answered unless it was understood and approved by...the average depositor.
>
> This caused me to sit down at my desk and try to visualize the types representative of the overwhelming majority. I tried to picture a mason, at work on a new building, a girl behind a counter and a farmer in the field. Perhaps my thoughts went back to this kind of individual citizen whom I have known so well in Dutchess County all my life. The net result was the dictation of a radio talk to these people-all of whom had their little capital or savings in some kind of bank...."[24]

By December of 1933 government public works projects had expanded, providing jobs for the thousands of unemployed. DCHS Board members began exploring ways in which such programs might help locally with their own mission. They pursued the possibility of using a Civil Works Administration (CWA) program to continue an ongoing project of several years duration—copying and cataloguing marriage and death notices in newspapers at Adriance Library. Up until then the project had been handled by Society volunteers under Miss Reynolds' supervision. Mr. Mylod and Miss Reynolds were given responsibility for pursuing the CWA program's ability to provide salaries for five clerk-typists supervised by DCHS and using space provided by Adriance Library. Information in letters exchanged between Reynolds and FDR that month (President's Personal File at FDR Library) and in the minutes in the 1933 Year

Book show the progress of planning. At length, it was learned that Adriance would have to be the lead agency because DCHS was not a tax supported institution. Nonetheless the project continued successfully under DCHS supervision from 1934 to 1939.

In her letter of December 6, 1933 to the President, Reynolds proposed an idea floated initially by Henry Hackett, who had become a DCHS Trustee:

> You know you promised last January that when in Washington you were tired you would relax by 'playing' with local history. Well, yesterday, Henry Hackett said to me how wonderful it would be if, now, in your present position, you could get from London copies of the logs of ships that came up the Hudson in 1777. Henry thinks those ship-records would have detailed entries of the places fired at, what observations were made, etc.
>
> I replied: yes, and then perhaps the data could be printed in the Year Book! Henry has been made a trustee of the DCHS and is taking an active interest. He has picked up an old copy of the Calendar of New York Land Papers and says he has found in it something of special interest about the Crooke water-lots (yours) and will give me the page numbers so I can check the items. I will send them to you if they are new to you and me...."[25]

As a lover of both local history and anything to do with naval history, FDR was enchanted with the idea. He immediately set in motion the wheels of government to locate the documents requested. In 1934 the search began. The 1935 Year Book shows the results in copies of the first batch of "Traveled Documents Presented to the Dutchess County Historical Society by the President of the United States," found in Canadian Archives through the efforts of the Honorable Warren Delano Robbins, then (1934) Minister to Canada. FDR "played" with history by assisting the search and depositing the document copies—which he enjoyed reading—with the Society. The 1935 Year Book also included 'Events on Hudson's River in 1777 as Recorded by British Officers in Contemporary

Reports.*"*These copies came with the cooperation of the British Admiralty through the intercession of our Ambassador from the United States to the Court of St. James, the Honorable Robert W. Bingham. These copies were also deposited with the Society by the President.

The search for related documents in other nation's archives revealed so many wonderful treasures that Miss Reynolds had enough for yet another Year Book article in 1936, the second installment of "Events on Hudson's River in 1777."

The year1936 found FDR campaigning again for a second term. His correspondence with Miss Reynolds continued unabated, with favors traded back and forth and invitations extended by FDR and Eleanor to visit Washington. She managed visits to Hyde Park with help from the President who arranged with his secretary, Missy Lehand, "to have a car come pick her up." It was often an open invitation to include others of her associates that he might also wish to see such as Dr. Poucher, or Amy Pearce Ver Nooy, DCHS Assistant Secretary and Reynolds's trusted protégé. Invitations to Washington were tempting but had to be declined because of the expense. After declining many times, Miss Reynolds finally spent the 1937 Easter holiday with them at the White House. It was the thrill of her life, as evidenced by comments in her letter of April 7, 1937:

> Dear Mr. President,
> …At the Congressional Library I had two most satisfactory interviews with the Chief of the Map Division, Colonel Lawrence Martin. Hereafter, he will I think be on the watch for material in regard to Dutchess County and our river.

It is to be noted that Col. Martin was the brother of Mr. George Martin of the Bureau of Geographic Names. This may refer to the clarification of Kromme Elleboog/Crum Elbow as a place name listed as an official decision of the U.S. Board on Geographical Names—a board within the Department of Interior- on April 29, 1937 as "Names in Dutchess County, New York."

Reynolds had a wonderful time digging through new documentary source-fields, ending her letter with thoughts of the hope of returning.

> And how I would love to go again! You gave me such a truly enjoyable time, for which I can't thank you enough. For over four years of illness, finances and home duties have held me a prisoner in one spot and you can have no idea of what it meant to me to get a glimpse into the world of people and events. I shall have something to feed on mentally for some time to come…."
> Sincerely your friend, Helen Wilkinson Reynolds

After 1937, FDR, in his second term was making great progress institutionalizing his new ideas. Public works utilizing history, culture, and art would emerge nation-wide until the start of World War II. Reynolds and her associates in the Society and the community were called upon almost daily over the next few years to provide historical background and architectural commentary on local projects such as the new post offices in a number of Dutchess County municipalities. Her work guiding Gerald Foster and the other muralists for the Poughkeepsie Post Office would be one of FDR's proudest achievements, followed by Olin Dows' paintings and Reynolds' research for the Hyde Park and Rhinebeck structures. She wrote to FDR supporting DCHS President W. Willis Reese's ideas for the Wappingers Post Office murals. They were based in part upon the recorded journal of the Marquis De Chastellux—his revolutionary era impressions of the falls—and in part on a view of the industrialized Great Falls in the early 19th century. The impact of this Reynolds' note to FDR returns in the record as a memo, November 2, 1939, from the president to Ned Bruce, where project oversight lay, in essence approving of the ideas. And so they were painted. Public cornerstone layings and formal openings of these monuments to history became celebrations in and of themselves and an opportunity for all the history friends to take a bow and be listed in commemorative programs. Like the stained glass windows in medieval gothic churches that taught biblical history, these paintings would bring local history to life for generations of Dutchess County residents and their children far into the future.

The death of Miss Reynolds's beloved mother, her companion and dearest friend, in the winter of 1938 was a blow that took a heavy toll. It came during the period when, as County Historian, and DCHS Trustee, she was deeply immersed in planning for Poughkeepsie's 150th celebration of New York's Ratification of the United States Constitution, ratified in the County Courthouse here, on July 26, 1788. Her grief and the strain of work, alleviated only in part by a sensitively worded sympathy letter from the President, proved too much of a burden. She wisely took herself off to a local sanitarium for a rest, trusting to Amy Pearce Ver Nooy, with FDR's approval, the continued daily research and transcription tasks on work that he had initiated or requested.

The commemoration was important to the President as well, for this was the moment in history in which his great-great grandfather Isaac voted *for* ratification. In her room in the private hospital, Reynolds came into possession of a state legislative committee memo (not intended for her viewing) outlining plans for the commemoration and indicating that the bulk of money appropriated for the celebration would be spent in Albany. It was apparent that little help would come to Poughkeepsie. It greatly upset her. The chair of the legislative committee charged with the planning was Irwin Steingut. She saw that lobbying would be essential by homesite interests for a proper event to be realized. Her first instinct was to enlist FDR, who was more adept at political intrigue than she. Without her typewriter- left at home when she entered the sanitarium-she wrote apologetically to him on a hospital pad, sharing the details of her inadvertent espionage and seeking his help.[26]

Miss Reynolds, aided by DCHS board members and local political friends, lobbied Albany for funds to make the celebration an important statement about New York's role in building the nation. A proposal for an organization to guide the planning envisioned joining national, state and local interests with an Honorary Committee composed of FDR, Governor Lehman, state legislators

Irwin Steingut and Frederick Bontecue and DCHS's Dr. Poucher. The local chair proposed would be Mayor George Spratt assisted by an Executive Committee including Dr. Baldwin and local officials: G. Russell Lozier, William Duggan and Raymond Guernsey, plus an unnamed Executive Secretary to the committee who would be paid $500. With a slight prod from FDR, the Honorable Irwin Steingut made certain that sufficient funds—$5000 of a total of $30,000—were made available for Poughkeepsie. All summer letters flowing between Reynolds and FDR spelled out the progress of trying to plan a local celebration in which he might participate. It was deferred until fall when all the school children could be involved in the hopes that he could fit it into an increasingly tight schedule. Her disappointment with the difficulties of complying with his schedule for even a fall date was evident. As an alternative, he sought his mother Sara's support to open Springwood for a visit from participants in a joint meeting of DCHS and the New York State Historical Association. The Fall Pilgrimage of the Society was joined to the Ratification plans and made a part of the New York State Historical Association's convention at Vassar, planned with Dr. James Baldwin's assistance. On September 16 a line of 150 or more cars, holding more than 450 persons, motored north along Route 9, a route interpreted in a printed program by Reynolds, for a drive through Springwood grounds and a view of the President's "private estate" and on to the former Bard/then Vanderbilt Estate, to St. James Church, where the President was then a Senior Warden, to end at a reception at Montgomery Place in Red Hook.

From Idea to Reality—A Storehouse for History Treasures

By 1938, Roosevelt's plans for his Presidential Library and its contents had begun to crystallize. The impact of his interest in gathering family and property-related materials is evident in correspondence showing his dependence upon Reynolds and her team of miners to unearth such materials. Her hand-written letter to him only a day after the exhausting Poughkeepsie celebration was history briefly referred to the event's success and her gratitude for his help. She got on immediately to the next piece of business: unearthing documents and collecting. George S. Van Vliet had uncovered an original record book of Crum Elbow Precinct in the Adriance Library and he had in his possession a survey map of the Crum Elbow riverfront and Point. A note affixed to the letter by FDR for Missy LeHand indicated his interest: "I want this at Hyde Park when I go up-FDR.[27]

Roosevelt arranged once again with Missy for a car to pick up Reynolds, Amy Ver Nooy and Dr. Poucher at Adriance Library when he would be in Hyde Park. On this occasion the visitors also included, with his blessing, Miss Guernsey of the library staff.

Such visits were not uncommon. Reynolds' notes to his mother, Sara, indicate that the two communicated easily and that Mrs. Roosevelt was happy to be her son's emissary for package and note delivery and as a surrogate hostess to the Historical Society circle of acquaintances in his absence. Reynolds also was in friendly communication with the Rosedale Estate Roosevelts, Ellie and Grace, with whom she frequently met. On more than one occasion it was as FDR's agent, as an interested party in family historical materials in their possession.

Reynolds's missives to Washington, like those of Daisy Suckley, were speedily delivered to the President. The envelopes, saved with the correspondence in the FDR Library, were marked especially for hand delivery to FDR *("Attention, Miss Le Hand, Personal")*. LeHand was his personal secretary from 1920 until a stroke in the summer of 1941 made it impossible for her to carry out her duties. Thereafter, Grace Tully was the delivery person.[28]

Helen Reynolds and her team were as intimately involved in the Library planning process as was Daisy Suckley. The President's letter to Reynolds of December 13 1938 is evidence that substantive discussions had been ongoing for some time.

> Dear Helen:
>   Many thanks for your note. I was sure that you would
>   be deeply interested. And strictly between ourselves, for

the time being, I wonder what you would think of the following:

Of course, I have relatively little Dutchess County material but there are a number of pictures, books and manuscripts—hardly enough to justify a Dutchess County Room in the new building. There is enough material, however, pictures, books, etc., if we include the Hudson Valley, to occupy an entire room. What would you think of the possibility of a Hudson River room and a separate Dutchess County room, the latter to contain such collections of the Dutchess County Historical Society as it might care to deposit there? I am sure this could be worked out with the National Archives and would give the D.C.H.S. (sic) a place to display to the public any pictures, etc., that are of real public interest. Also the room could serve as a meeting place for the Executive Committee of the building and a gathering place for the pilgrimages of the Society[29]

If we could have our own building for the Society in Poughkeepsie, of course, it would be a wonderful thing, but I see no prospect of getting money for such a building or of being able to maintain one if we had it.

What do you think?

As ever yours,

Franklin D. Roosevelt

By return mail Reynolds sent FDR a copy of the press releases and editorial in Poughkeepsie's *The Evening Star*, December 12 and 13[h] 1938, announcing the plan to open the museum in Hyde Park. It was obviously no surprise to her. What is surprising to this generation in the articles is the interest reported from county government leaders such as County Clerk Frederic A. Smith, who is reported as seeing this as an opportunity to place all of the County's archival records there, as well as some which had already been removed to Adriance by the lobbying efforts of Miss Reynolds and John J. Mylod. The December 12th editorial bewailed the fact that the County, then as now, had no museum of its own and encouraged County, Adriance, and Roosevelt cooperation to build a major public institution accessible to all. The editorial appealed to a generous public to support the library with a fund drive… "Why not a campaign to aid in the creation of the museum with perhaps a dollar as the largest contribution, that all might participate?"

Reynold's hand-written letter to FDR of December 20, 1938 just before Christmas, states in part:

> Before me lie your letters of December 13th and 15th, the former bearing upon the possibility of a Dutchess County Room in the archives building at Hyde Park and the latter upon the record book of the Little Nine Partners Preparative Meeting. The record book arrived safely by parcel post. …I will hold the Little Nine Partners book until then also (*until she returned home from a visit to New Jersey cousins*) in order not to risk it in the crowded mails of the next few days….
> Your old friend, Helen[30]

She was privy to his thinking and was doing some of her own on the subject. She had in her possession materials he coveted. Continued references to planning, items to be sought—or in hand—fill correspondence over the next few years. For each of them this work with history was "play"—a term that appeared often in their correspondence.

The 1939 Year Book announced that publication was underway of a limited edition of Volume VII of DCHS's Occasional Publications—*Records of the Crum Elbow Precinct, Dutchess County*, edited by Franklin D. Roosevelt. The cost would be $10 and Dr. Poucher was the contact for those interested in assuring themselves a copy. One wonders just when FDR had time to fit this task into a 1939 presidential schedule that included dealing with the World's Fair in New York City, the visit of the British Royal Family, an unsettling array of international problems added to national issues, and an up-coming election. Editing the documents undoubtedly *was* his relaxation—the "play"—to which Reynolds often referred and felt that he deserved.

When illness took Reynolds back to the sanitarium in February of 1939 Ver Nooy and Poucher filled in for her, handling the details of getting the book printed and keeping the lines of communication open with the President with regard to document searches. FDR's nose for collectible investments and his parsimonious streak are also apparent in the correspondence that year.[31] Despite her illness, Reynolds & Company made certain that FDR got his money's worth, whether it meant comparing printers' prices or dickering with antiquarians and document owners in an effort to get the best price for a purchase or an outright gift for FDR's Library. Eventually, one hundred fifty copies of his book on Crum Elbow Records were printed by a Poughkeepsie printer, Lansing Broas, and made available by 1940. Those who bought it made a wise investment in a rare book.

Through the summer and fall of 1939 plans for the Dutchess Room took shape and it is obvious that FDR was trying to find a way to get it paid for that would allow "an endowment" fund for paying a curator.

From aboard the U.S.S. *Tuscaloosa* on August 21, 1939, he wrote to Reynolds in detail about his interest in making "the Dutchess County Historical Society room (sic) in the new Library a repository or depository (which is it?) (sic) for the town and church records and privately owned material." That same letter foresees "one person to have charge of the collections... " He had been pondering how to go about mixing federal archives and material culture collections with those owned by a local organization; not only how to structure the administration but how to keep them separate and pay for care of the local history collection. His plan included Reynolds..."but I should greatly like to have the Dutchess County historical material itself under the supervision of one of our own people—preferably H.W.R." [32]

His letters were full of history questions for her to answer. Though ill and fatigued she did her best to send him the information he needed as attachments to a letter telling him that she would have to defer a decision about the curatorial position until her health improved.[33]

She was well enough however to make it to the cornerstone

laying of the Library in November and made certain that she and Poucher got there, despite a car accident that had laid him low, interfering with his driving, and despite the possibility of more surgery for her own spinal problems. She asked the President to add Dr. Baldwin to the guest list so they would have a ride and got her wish.[34]

December 1939 found Reynolds fretting about a check for $10 she had sent as a contribution to the Library fund. Missy LeHand made it her business to track it down. It now resides in the Library archives along with Helen's note and messages from FDR re the loss of her gift—which he knew was a great deal for one in her limited circumstances.

As Library construction progressed, the President's interest in pinning down a collection and staff for the Dutchess Room became focused on minute details, usually the business of museum professional staff. He was much concerned with appropriate materials for exhibits; engravings, manuscripts, the Civil War draft wheel and articles of clothing seemed most interesting to him. He thought such items might occupy "three or four glass cases and be changed from time to time to prevent fading." He thought that the basement could be used for large items, which might include the Suckley 1810 carriage.[35] At this point his meetings with Miss Reynolds often included Mrs. Ver Nooy, upon whom Reynolds had become greatly dependent as physical and emotional exhaustion took its toll.

FDR understood what was happening and by the end of April 1940 began to develop a new strategy, which expanded his relationship through correspondence with Ver Nooy and opened a serious discussion on the issue of future Dutchess Room staffing with both women. His letter of April 20, 1940, got right down to the business of salaries, positions and duties for Reynolds, Ver Nooy and also Daisy Suckley. He had found a $2000 position line in the National Archives budget that he fancied dividing three ways:

• Reynolds as senior administration of the Dutchess and Hudson Valley collections, twelve days a year for $100, (He wanted her knowledge and oversight as a guide.)

• Suckley as his special agent seeking materials for the collection in the area, one day a week throughout the year for $400, and

• Mrs. Ver Nooy as curatorial staff on site, under Civil Service, for the remaining $1500.

He asked Helen to do some checking on Ver Nooy's current salary at Adriance to determine if this would work. He also suggested that if Helen still insisted upon making that donation (the lost check), she should send it to Mr. Frank C. Walker and designate it for cases for the Dutchess Room.[36]

Her response to him was undoubtedly a most painful letter to write. Her ethical but sensitive reply was that, as a member of the Adriance Board of Trustees, the governing body of the institution for whom Mrs. Ver Nooy worked, she was under oath to see to that institution's best interests.[37] She suggested that she be taken out of the equation, and then wrote a generous reference to her friend FDR for her friend Amy Pearce Ver Nooy, with whom she (HWR) felt he should deal directly.

This awkward phase of the relationship moved easily back to one of friendly helpfulness. Reynolds, in answer to a prospective offer of materials to DCHS's collections, referred to her by the Archivist of the United States, responded that the Society did not purchase items. She suggested instead that the offer be made to the FDR Library.[38]

The identification of a variety of materials suitable to be collected for the Library continued amicably and on June 29, 1940 Reynolds received a presidential invitation to attend a luncheon preceding the formal ceremony turning the Library over to the government on Thursday, July 4 1940.

Missy also dropped a note on September 6, 1940 to Amy Ver Nooy, in her role as DCHS's Assistant Secretary, to pass along the President's thought that she (Ver Nooy) should not send a $10 copy of his book (*The Records of Crum Elbow Precinct*) to *The New York Times,* "as he thinks it will soon be forgotten." FDR's staff had tried to reach her by telephone but she was on vacation.[39] Ver

Nooy's competent attention to the final proofing of his Crum Elbow records book and the handling of the modest financial arrangements between him and the Society pleased FDR. He asked Missy to tell her that he was "delighted with the book and appreciates what she has done." He added to Missy, "Deposit the $92 (return on sales) in the Guarantee Trust. "[40] Such human touches in the correspondence put a different light on the character of national leadership. He did, indeed, attend to details.

His friends in the Dutchess County Historical Society continued to do him favors and keep his mind off the burdens of office briefly for the few remaining years that were left to him. His dependency on Helen Reynolds to get to the bottom of research problems is clear in every letter between them: concern over what might happen to Grace and Ellie Roosevelt's "tin box" of papers—Would they accept $250 for them to go to the Library? Could she track down a relative of Ed Platt to see if letters of Isaac Roosevelt's that Ed had borrowed when he wrote the Poughkeepsie history book could be found?[41] Every communiqué includes, in part, new inquiries and/or the status of ongoing investigations ranging from concerns about local Stoutenburgh records and Braman materials, to hints about the location and availability of copies of maps, documents, paintings, etc…

Reynolds grew more frail and concern for her presidential friend during the election of 1940 was the final straw, sending her back to the sanitarium until spring of 1941. The President's health had also suffered under the strain of politics and international problems. Short notes of good wishes cheered them both. FDR gained her thanks by staffing the Library with persons of whom she approved, e.g. Allen Frost, who also served as DCHS curator, as a Junior Museum Aide, and Fred Shipman the Library Director, with whom she was discussing ideas certain to excite the president. She was sad to miss the formal opening of the Library, scheduled during her vacation on Martha's Vineyard. FDR urged another visit to Washington D.C. She reported on the progress of Olin Dows' murals and urged the president to "play" more with history.

The start of World War II on December 7, 1941 would end any thought of visits and send DCHS, like all other American institutions, into a wartime stance. Nonetheless, during the coming year FDR continued to fret about Grace and Ellie's sales of materials to dealers and asked Helen to urge them to talk to him before selling anything. For once, his hold on the purse strings loosened.[42]

The End of an Era

On May 11, 1942, for the last time until the end of the war, DCHS members enjoyed a short trip in conjunction with the spring meeting, held at the new Library. A talk by Olin Dows on his murals for Hyde Park and Rhinebeck post offices shared his perspectives on public art with an appreciative audience. They matched those of FDR and Reynolds in his expressed views: "Our knowledge of history comes largely through art. Great art is a living record. It galvanizes cold facts… Most important, it helps form and shape our beliefs." Delighted DCHS members then were turned over to farmer and scholar Benjamin Haviland, who had become one of Roosevelt's favorite local resource persons when it came to the history of his hometown. Haviland, who on FDR's recommendation had taken his place as Town Historian, conducted the members on a tour of the hamlet with an overview of land ownership, old families and development from the 17th century. Then it was on to the president's new retreat—Top Cottage.

During a period when Hyde Park sites were protected by armed military police, delighted DCHS members wandered unhampered through the grounds and the President's private hide-away cottage, as his special guests. A letter to him that week from Reynolds reported on her regular conferences with Daisy Suckley, with whom she worked comfortably, and sent details of the DCHS visit to his cottage. She enclosed a Bird's Foot Violet picked by Edith A. Roberts, a Vassar faculty member and friend with whom she had written *The Role of Plant Life in Dutchess County.*[43] The President responded to her disappointment that he could not be present, explaining that "If I went to even the smallest kind of public gathering the papers would have to print that I was at Hyde Park. You will be amused to know that I am now a battleship—my movements cannot be printed." He ended the letter with hopes of being home for a whole week soon, to which he appended a hand written note. "I will see you then."[44]

Their letters, full of discoveries and advice, continued as the war raged in Europe and the Pacific. In November she wrote the president with pleasure about her discovery of materials in the Kansas City Library relating to Associate Supreme Court Justice Smith Thompson which she knew would interest him.[45] One of her last letters, written December 5, 1942, was to thank him for *The True Story of Fala*, Daisy Suckley's charming tale about FDR's beloved Scottie. She was ill again but did not wish to worry him by silence, so encouraged him to keep in touch at her "war time" home—56 Grand Avenue in Poughkeepsie. Her illness was more serious than she cared to admit even to herself.

The friendship that began with a mutual interest in local history ended on January 3, 1943 with Helen Reynolds' unexpected death. Her friend Edith Roberts bore the burden of delivering the message to her friend FDR. She telegraphed the President that evening: "Helen passed away peacefully at 5:30 today—Edith A. Roberts."

He, in return, telegraphed Miss Roberts his deepest sympathy, but those who understood the depth of the friendship between the two realized that it was the President who was more in need of comfort. Maud Stoutenburgh Eliot, with whom Reynolds had worked on FDR's behalf researching Hyde Park's beginnings through its 18th century Stoutenburgh family records was among those who sent the President her condolences and received a personal reply:

> "It is a real tragedy about Helen Reynolds. She was a grand friend and we had worked together so much on things relating to Dutchess County that I shall greatly miss her. And so much remains to be done—with nobody to take her place...."

Indeed, there was no *one* to take her place, particularly with the

President. His interest in local history languished as the war took its toll on his time and health and made him even more a prisoner of his office. One of his favorite correspondents was no longer sending him local history mysteries to "play" with. Replacing her would take *many* willing workers.

Epilogue

Minutes of the Dutchess County Historical Society through the remaining war years show how hard the other members of the "Reynolds & Company" team worked to keep up the pace that she had set. Between March 1942 and January 1943 DCHS had lost not only the leadership of Reynolds, but also that of Society President W. Willis Reese who had been killed in a March 28, 1942 accident. One of her last sad duties was to help compose his formal memorial and to write Society condolences to the family.

Her diminishing energies during 1942 had been spent to urge board members to hold fast during this difficult time when many of the normal functions of the Society, such as its Pilgrimages, would have to be suspended for the duration of the war. Fuel shortages, rationing and salvage collection programs affected everyone. Labor and volunteer shortages found everyone, young and old, pressed into service. Government attempts to salvage all materials useable for the war reached into every corner. A message on this subject sent to DCHS's semi-annual meeting on October 16, 1942 by Governor Lehman came with the caveat that in gathering reusable goods for war production everyone should take care not to destroy valuable historical materials. He cautioned the public to place such items safely in the hands of local historical societies or libraries. The government's Committee on Conservation of Cultural Resources urged these agencies to place important materials in vaults where they would be safe. DCHS, with no vault, through its curator, Allen Frost, arranged to move collections materials from Vassar Institute to the FDR Library vaults for safekeeping for the remainder of the conflict.

Barely a month before her death, despite her illness, Reynolds had completed work on her final Year Book for publication and worked with the nominating committee to fill the ranks of DCHS trustee leadership, little knowing that hers would be the next empty place.

The Minutes of the February 10 meeting of the Trustees in 1943, a month after her death, expressed the loss of a dear friend and colleague in a resolution composed by her former co-workers Dr. Poucher, George S. Van Vliet and Mrs. Waterman. Helen's protégé, Amy Ver Nooy, was assigned the editorial duties for the next Year Book; Harry Harkness Flagler was appointed to fill her position on the board and discussion began of a proper memorial to her.

Dr. Poucher and Dr. Baldwin wrote their tribute to a dear friend and colleague: In part it expressed their very personal feelings:

> To win her commendation was a high honor, for her critical abilities were keen; but even the novice could be sure of a kindly hearing. To me (sic) this dear lady and gifted historian is a precious memory. May her name never be forgotten in the county of her delight.…

During the remaining years of the war DCHS leadership changes came quickly, with a loss of older members to death and younger members to war duties. Olin Dows was among its leadership—eleven men and one woman—pressed into military service. Older DCHS members, such as Allen Frost did double duty in their retirement years. He served as an FDR Library Museum Aide, contributing to the protection of national cultural resources that so concerned Governor Lehman. He regularly urged the Society, as had Reynolds, to identify safer storage for its collections. His report to the Trustees at their 1943 meetings outlined the efforts of the FDR Library to microfilm important large collections, e.g., the Bard, Rogers Family and Levi P. Morton papers at the Library, as a protective measure against loss. He urged the trustees to allow their materials to be filmed also, when the Library was prepared to do so. In 1944 Edgar Nixon of the FDR Library reported to Society members at the October 21 Semi-Annual meeting that microfilming of county documents was finally underway. That same year's Annual Meeting Minutes reported the formal gift by FDR to DCHS of documents used by him for articles in earlier Year Books.

The "Our President Says" report in the 1944 Year Book by Raymond G. Guernsey reports the official designation of a Helen Wilkinson Reynolds Fund. Although a final decision had not yet been made for use of the fund, President Guernsey's letter to members echoed both her teachings and Frost's concerns: "We look forward to the time when we shall have a permanent home for our valuables, particularly a fireproof and air-conditioned vault. Some of our documents and possessions are housed in Vassar Brothers Institute and others are temporarily at the FDR Library…let each of us pledge his or her utmost to the advancement of the Dutchess County Historical Society. "

In the Spring of 1945, barely four months into his historic fourth term, Franklin D. Roosevelt died, a victim of the war as much as any soldier on the battlefield. The mourners in Dutchess County felt a personal loss as deep as the passing of a cherished family member.

The full memorial resolution from the Trustees was presented to DCHS members on page 21 of the 1946 Year Book. It was prepared for board approval by Clara Steeholm, Henry T. Hackett (Roosevelt's lawyer and friend) and Frank V. Mylod (John J. Mylod's son and one of the new generation of DCHS leaders). In part, its clauses summarize a familial relationship of more than thirty years:

> "WHEREAS, on April 12, 1945, Franklin Delano Roosevelt, the thirty-first President of the United States, died at Warm Springs, Georgia, having been a member of the Dutchess County Historical Society from the time of its organization in 1914 and Vice-President for the Town of Hyde Park since 1926, and
> WHEREAS, he was an ardent and enthusiastic student of Dutchess County history and always took a deep interest

in the activities of this Society, contributing material for the Year Books and editing publications under its auspices, and

WHEREAS, while Governor of New York State and President of the United States, he frequently used his influence to procure for the Society articles of historical value which were not readily obtainable…"

"…this Society appreciates the great honor of having had him as a member for so many years and owes him a deep sense of gratitude for his work and efforts in promoting and aiding in its work…"

"…this Society records his passing with profound sorrow, for he was its most distinguished and illustrious member, and extends to his family its expression of sympathy and respect.

When Allen Frost (1877-1946) died in May of the next year his memorial noted the importance of his work as collector and caretaker safeguarding a great variety and volume of local history materials. It stated: "…in his desk in the Franklin D. Roosevelt Library, named and classified with admirable skill, may be found the lists of hundreds of documents…"[46] The lessons taught by FDR and the key members of the "Reynolds & Company" project team had successfully filtered throughout the leadership and membership of the Society and become their watch word. Those who followed would now better understand the responsibilities of saving, collecting, caring for and making accessible the historical record of the community and valley. The team left behind a stronger, more professional local history keepers' organization and helped to build the first of the nation's presidential libraries.

Roosevelt and Reynolds left a legacy of ideas, actions and completed work in the hands of colleagues of their generation who continued their work, made it their own and passed it along to the next generation. Indiana Jones' fictional achievements pale beside the real successes of a local hero and heroine whose greatest gift to us was an accessible, truthful memory of our past.

NOTES

1. It was a family tradition to bestow the name of paternal ancestors every other generation, e.g., Isaac (1726-1794-NYC, Barrytown/RedHook), James (1760-1847-Poughkeepsie), Dr. Isaac (1790-1863-Hyde Park), James (1828-1900-Poughkeepsie/Hyde Park).

2. Geoffrey C. Ward, *Before the Trumpet*, (New York, Harper and Rowe, Publishers,, 1985), p. 158.

3. Ibid., p. 250.

4. *Year Book of the Dutchess County Historical Society, May 1914-April 1915*, p.6.

5. *Year Book of the Dutchess County Historical Society, October 1915-Oct. 1916*, p.3.

6. *Year Book of the Dutchess County Historical Society, May 1914-April 1915*, p. 25.

7. *Year Book of the Dutchess County Historical Society, 1924*, Minutes of Trustees, Feb. 11, 1924, p. 9. Descriptions of the books are listed on p. 30.

8. Miss Reynolds to Franklin Roosevelt, Sept. 24, 1924, FDR Library, Reynolds Correspondence, Box 113.

9. DCHS began publishing its Year Book series in 1914-1915. Other books and booklets outside this annual series were called "Occasional Publications." FDR's contributions were among this body of published works.

10. *Year Book of the Dutchess County Historical Society, Volume 27, 1942*. Annual Report, Treasurer, Dutchess County Historical Society, May 11, 1942. p. 21.

11. *Year Book of the Dutchess County Historical Society, 1923*. p. 34.

12. *Year Book of the Dutchess County Historical Society, 1924*. Semi-Annual Meeting minutes, Oct. 18, 1923. p. 7.

13. Ghee and Spence. "The Taconic State Parkway." *Taconic Pathways Through Beekman, Union Vale, LaGrange, Washington and Stanford*. (Charleston, SC, Arcadia Publishing, 2000.) pp. 9-16.

14. Ibid., p.30.

15. *Year Book of the Dutchess County Historical Society, 1927*. pp. 28, 29.

16. Miss Reynolds to FDR, Nov. 24, 1929. Box 67, Governor's Papers, FDRL.

17. Reynolds to FDR, October 3, 1924. FDR to Reynolds, Oct. 13, 1931. Op cit. FDRL.

18. This article clipping is attached to Helen Reynold's personal copy of the 1931 Year Book in the collections of the Dutchess County Historical Society—J. Ghee.

19. Reynolds to FDR, Nov. 13, 1932. FDR to Reynolds, November 18, 1932. Governor's Papers, FDRL.

20. Reynolds to FDR, April 1, 1933. President's Personal File, box 234, FDRL.

21. FDR to Reynolds, April 5, 1933. President's Personal File, box 234, FDRL.

22. Frank Friedel, *FDR Launching the New Deal*, (Boston-Toronto, Little, Brown and Company, 1973.) Friedel covers FDR's first year in office, his accomplishments and challenges, week by week and issue by issue.

23. *Year Book of the Dutchess County Historical Society*, Vol. 18, 1933. "Kromme Elleboog Seventeenth Century Place-Name in the Hudson Valley." P. 58-68.

24. Ibid., pp. 35, 36

25. Reynolds to FDR, December 6, 1933. President's Personal File, box 234, FDRL.

26. Reynolds to FDR, March 25, 1938, President's Personal File, box 234, FDRL.

27. Reynolds to FDR/FDR affixed note, September 19, 1938, PPF, box 234, FDRL.

28. Grace Tully, *F.D.R., My Boss* (Chicago, Ill., Chas. Scribner's Sons, 1949), pp 245-246.

29. From 1981, when I was appointed Dutchess County Historian, until I left office in 1991, at the urging of Dr. William Emerson, Director of the FDR Library, this tradition of using the Dutchess County Room as a gathering place for local historians was revived in joint conferences with my office and in annual meetings of the Dutchess County Municipal Historian's Association—J. Ghee.

30. Reynolds to FDR, December 20, 1938, PPF, box 234. FDRL

31. Correspondence Reynolds and FDR, January-August 1939, PPF, FDRL.

32. FDR to Reynolds, August 21, 1939, PPF, box 234, FDRL.

33. Reynolds to FDR, August 29, 1939, PPF, box 234, FDRL.

34. Reynolds to FDR , Nov. 3, 1939, PPF, box 234, FDRL.

35. FDR to Reynolds, March 21, 1940, PPF, box 234, FDRL.

36. FDR to Reynolds, April 20, 1940 from Warm Springs, GA. PPF, box 234, FDRL.

37. Reynolds to FDR, April 29, 1940, PPF, box 234, FDRL.

38. Reynolds to R. W.W. Connor, May 17, 1940, PPF, box 234, FDRL.

39. LeHand to VerNooy, September 6, 1940, PPF, box 234, FDRL.

40. FDR to LeHand, Memo of 12-23-40, FDRL.

41. FDR to Reynolds, December 27, 1940, PPF box 234, FDRL.

42. FDR to Reynolds, February 9, 1942, PPF box 234, FDRL.

43. Reynolds to FDR, May 13, 1942, PPF, box 234, FDRL. *The Role of Plant Life in Dutchess County* was a joint project of Vassar College botanist Edith Adelaide Roberts and Miss Reynolds, supported by Vassar funding and published in 1938.

44. FDR to Reynolds, May 18, 1942, PPF, box 234, FDRL.

45. Reynolds to FDR, Nov. 5, 1942, PPF, box 234, FDRL.

46. *Year Book of The Dutchess County Historical Society, 1946*, p. 14.

Five Dutch Colonial Post Offices

Bernice L. Thomas

Five post offices in Dutchess County built between 1936 and 1940 in Beacon, Poughkeepsie, Rhinebeck, Wappingers Falls and Hyde Park, and a sixth in Ellenville in Ulster County, stand out as a distinctive group among the 1,100 new post offices built during the Roosevelt New Deal. The post offices are essentially a Dutchess County phenomenon; the comparable one in Ulster County was the result of a request for a post office like the one in Rhinebeck.

The time was right for new post offices in Dutchess County. They were a part of a federal program of public works to give employment to Americans during the Great Depression. Moreover, they were part of a campaign to improve the quality of federal architecture. The person most responsible for both these endeavors was a resident of Dutchess County, President Franklin D. Roosevelt. It was the President who wanted post offices distinguished by their architecture in these communities.

Post offices were the special domain of another Dutchess County resident: Secretary of the Treasury Henry J. Morgenthau, Jr., who shared Roosevelt's goal of better public architecture, as well as his affection for Dutchess County. In his address at the laying of the

Bernice L. Thomas is a Vassar graduate with a M.A. and Ph.D in Art History from Boston University. She moved to Poughkeepsie in 1999 to write a book entitled The Stamp of FDR: New Deal Post Offices in the Mid-Hudson Valley, *published in 2002 by Purple Mountain Press, Ltd. The material in this article comes from research for the book. An independent scholar, Thomas now lives in Albany, Georgia where she is pursuing a study of New Deal post offices in Southwest Georgia.*

Hyde Park Post Office, Rudolph Stanley-Brown architect. Photo: Bernice L. Thomas.

cornerstone for the Poughkeepsie Post Office in 1937, he noted that he took a special interest in this building because he was "a resident of Dutchess County and, like the rest of you, keenly interested in its history and traditions, as well as its present welfare."[1] As Secretary of the Treasury, Morgenthau could facilitate FDR's vision of fieldstone post offices in a Dutch Colonial style in Dutchess County. As a long-time friend and political ally of FDR, with a great deal in common, he was more than willing to do so.

The Roosevelts and the Morgenthaus were friends, often visiting each other at their respective country estates. Elinor Morgenthau played a critical role herself in the realization of the post offices. She acted as a go-between, apprising Treasury officials of the President's wishes. Eleanor Roosevelt also played a role, functioning as her husband's eyes and ears as she often did. In August 1936, she and Elinor Morgenthau drove to Woodstock, New York to check on the progress of Charles Rosen's mural for the post office in Beacon. The First Lady signaled her approval in her syndicated column "My Day," commenting on the lovely color and interesting design, along with "views which are historically interesting as well as scenically."[2] Sometime later she wrote about Olin Dows' murals in the Rhinebeck

Rhinebeck Post Office, Rudolph Stanley-Brown, architect. Photo: Bernice L. Thomas.

post office in her column: "…Every time I hear that people really get pleasure out of these paintings, which have an historical interest as well as an artistic one, I rejoice, for I feel that we are adding permanently to the cultural heritage of our country."[3] The two Dutchess County couples seemed to share a proprietary interest in the new fieldstone post offices and the way they were realized.

FDR dictated specific terms for the post office architecture. It must refer to a historic Dutch Colonial building in the locale and the buildings must be made of fieldstone, regardless of the historic model's original material. The fieldstone post office in Hyde Park, for instance, is based on an eighteenth-century wooden house of Dr. John Bard, whose estate gave its name to that community. Stones for the post office walls could be salvaged from historic ruins and other structures in the vicinity. The masonry of the stone walls should reflect the simplicity of pre-Revolutionary stone elevations. When the masonry of Eric Kebbon's Poughkeepsie Post Office seemed too sophisticated to FDR, he directed Treasury officials to send the architect up to Hyde Park to look at the James Roosevelt Memorial Library. The walls of this Dutch Colonial revival building, given by his mother in memory of his father in 1927, were evidently laid up

FDR and Henry Morgenthau, Jr. "To Elinor [Morgenthau] from one of two of a kind, Franklin D. Roosevelt," dated February 9, 1934. FDR PRESIDENTIAL LIBRARY

in a vernacular format satisfactory to the President.

President Roosevelt gave the wall decoration in the post office lobbies the same meticulous attention as the architecture. He approved the artists and the subject matter, which was to depict the life and history of each place. On occasion his choices were overridden, as when Roosevelt's advisor and Dutchess County historian, Helen Wilkinson Reynolds, suggested comparable scenes of mills on the falls in Wappingers Falls from 1780 and 1880 instead of views of the Wappinger Indians. Sometimes Roosevelt's choices were quite explicit, as when he put marks indicating "yes" and "no" beside a list of possible subjects for the Hyde Park Murals submitted to him personally by the muralist, Olin Dows. FDR asked to see artists' sketches as the work progressed and made corrections when he saw fit. The artist for a Poughkeepsie mural, Gerald Foster, was told to remove the horses from a scene in the forest showing an encounter between newly arrived Dutch settlers and Wappinger Indians in 1692. The President doubted if horses would have been there. Foster also

Hyde Park Post Office, Olin Dows mural of FDR and local school board reviewing plans for the new Franklin D. Roosevelt High School. BERNICE L. THOMAS

fattened some of the trees in the forest when Roosevelt, the tree farmer, objected that they looked like second growth.

The murals, reflective of life in Dutchess County, were integrated with the Dutch Colonial revival architecture. For example, Dr. John Bard, whose house was the model for the Hyde Park Post Office, is seen in a mural conferring with his son, Dr. Samuel Bard, about an agricultural experiment. This is particularly apt, since the building was officially a combination Agricultural Station and Post Office. Another example is the 1780 scene beside the Wappinger Falls which portrays Peter Mesier, an early owner of the Brouwer-Mesier House on which the design of the Wappingers Falls Post Office was based. The more one looks, the more one sees that there was a carefully orchestrated story embedded in the art and architecture of the post offices in this group.

One searches for reasons why FDR lavished so much attention on these post offices. They obviously relate to his deep interest in local history. This interest was manifested when he became a founding member of the Dutchess County Historical Society in 1915, and later when he served as Town Historian for Hyde Park. He also wrote about local history on occasion. Roosevelt was concerned about the fast disappearance of pre-Revolutionary Dutch Colonial buildings in the Hudson Valley. For him, post offices replicating selected historic buildings with related scenes painted on the walls inside were a form of historic preservation. It was his way of creating an enduring historic record. Future generations could see much of what he had known and loved in Dutchess County since he was a boy.

Roosevelt's interest in history extended to an interest in his own family history, and family history as it related to life in Dutchess County. The post office murals reflect this. An eighteenth century ancestor, Isaac Roosevelt, appears in a Poughkeepsie mural and again in a crowd scene in front of the Dutch Reformed Church in Rhinebeck. The latter appearance serves to confirm FDR's Dutch ancestry. The house of a cousin, Laura Delano, is pictured and noted in the text below in Rhinebeck as well. FDR's uncle, John Roosevelt, is shown with his iceboat on the Hudson River in Hyde Park. Roosevelt's father, James Roosevelt, appears in a Hyde Park mural, seated in his breaking cart at the Union Corners Racetrack in 1850. His mother and his wife are described in the wall text as being present on the porch of Top Cottage at the famous picnic for the King and Queen of England in 1939, although they are hard to decipher in the painting. They would have been seated on the porch of the Rhinebeck Post Office when it was dedicated a month before. However, the image of that ceremony over the exit is too small for anyone to be singled out.

A Dutchess County resident and Roosevelt family friend, Olin Dows, took a most unusual step, with the President's consent, and included FDR himself in the Hyde Park murals. He is shown as a young man clearing the woods for reforestation in 1905, and implied as his iceboat, *The Hawk*, sails out onto the river behind his Uncle John's boat in the foreground. Most significantly, FDR is pictured as the centerpiece of a contemporary scene going over architectural plans for the new Franklin D. Roosevelt High School with the Hyde Park School Board. He sits in his familiar open touring car, with his little dog Fala seated on the ground beside it. These are the only images of FDR in any New Deal post office mural anywhere in the United States. Greater evidence of his affinity with place is hard to imagine.

These post offices are a reflection of another consuming interest of FDR, architecture. Roosevelt considered himself an amateur architect and others did as well. Harlan Althen wrote an article entitled "F.D.R. as Architect" in the *New York Times Magazine* in 1940 in which he likened FDR and his avocation to that of another president, Thomas Jefferson.[4] Secretary Morgenthau made a similar observation in his address at the dedication of the Rhinebeck Post Office the year before. He called Roosevelt one of "two presidents who were sufficiently interested in architecture to suggest features of public buildings— and both of them with the happiest results." The other was Thomas Jefferson.[5] Roosevelt would sketch ground plans and elevations for a licensed architect to translate into architectural drawings. In a well-known anecdote, his personal architect, Henry J. Toombs, went so far as to sign drawings for Top Cottage, "Franklin D. Roosevelt, Architect," and "Henry J. Toombs, Associate." An abiding interest in architecture, and a strong preference for early Dutch architecture in the Hudson Valley account for a distinctive group of New Deal post offices built according to one man's specifications.

Another motivation for the post offices FDR oversaw in such detail was political. As he said at the dedication of the Franklin D. Roosevelt High School and two Hyde Park elementary schools in 1940, the schools "symbolize public works…built for the well-being of America."[6] Public works were the linchpin of the Roosevelt New Deal. A mural depicting the planning of Roosevelt High School could symbolize in perpetuity the benefits of the Roosevelt New Deal. An image of the new post office in Poughkeepsie in Charles Rosen's "View of the City of Poughkeepsie c. 1939" does much the same thing. The Mid-Hudson Bridge, so prominent in the same scene, serves to advertise Roosevelt's long-term commitment to public works, as the bridge opened when he was governor of New

York. Post Office murals at the service of politics are best illustrated in another Poughkeepsie mural by Gerald Foster: "July 26, 1788 New York State Ratifies the United States Constitution in the Dutchess County Court House in Poughkeepsie." The building itself referred back to an 1809 courthouse that had replaced the one where the action took place. Roosevelt's previously mentioned great-great grandfather, Isaac Roosevelt, figures prominently in the ratification scene. Gilbert Stuart's portrait of Isaac Roosevelt that held pride of place in the living room at Springwood served as the model. William Rhoads suggests that FDR's ancestor shown ratifying the United States Constitution was meant to carry a political message. The President was being accused of undermining the Constitution with his proposed New Deal programs. The image of his ancestor ratifying that document is visual proof of FDR's support of the United States Constitution.[7]

Roosevelt, the Dutchess County friend and neighbor, the amateur historian and architect, and Roosevelt, the astute politician, were interwoven in the formation of this unique group of New Deal post offices. Other Dutchess County residents were in the right place at the right time to support the President's intentions. It was a fertile moment that left a remarkable legacy to Dutchess County.

NOTES

1. Franklin Delano Roosevelt Library, *Morgenthau Diary*, v. 92, 58.

2. William B. Rhoads, "The Artistic Patronage of Franklin D. Roosevelt: Art as Historical Record," Prologue, Journal of the National Archives, 15 (1983): 4-21, 15.

3. FDR Library, Eleanor Roosevelt Papers, typed transcript of "My Day by Eleanor Roosevelt," copyright 1941.

4. Harlan Althen, "F.D.R. as Architect," *New York Times Magazine*, 8 December 1940, 9, 26.

5. "Morgenthau's Speech at Post Office," *Poughkeepsie Eagle News*, 2 May 1939, 9.

6. "Roosevelt Calls Our Free Schools a Bar to Tyranny," *The New York Times*, 6 October 1940, 1.

7. William B. Rhoads, "The President and the Sesquicentennial of the Constitution: Franklin Roosevelt's Monument in Poughkeepsie," *New York History* LVII (July 1990): 309-321. 321.

A President Goes Birding

James L. Whitehead

Once, when somebody complained to Eleanor Roosevelt that FDR had not spoken to him when he passed nearby, Mrs. Roosevelt replied that the President had blamed such incidents of the past on the fact that he was nearsighted—"but," she said, "that has always seemed strange to me, for, as long as I have known him, he could always identify any bird he happened to see."

Many people know, of course, that FDR loved birds and that, as a youngster in Hyde Park and as a schoolboy at Groton, he was a serious bird watcher and collector. What is not generally known is that he retained this interest in birds all his life. I happen to know that this is true, for I am one of five people who went with FDR on May 10, 1942, on the only bird watching trip, so far as we know, that he took either as President of the United States or, earlier, as Governor of New York. This does not indicate that he had lost interest. The President's daughter, Anna Roosevelt Halsted, told me in June 1975 that, although his public career and his polio ended most of his outdoor activities, her father often talked of birds and watched them whenever he had a chance—on picnics at Warm Springs, on drives through his Hyde Park woods, and even on cruises aboard U.S. Navy vessels, when he would use binoculars to look at other ships, distant shorelines, schools of fish—and birds.

Thus, when I joined the staff of the Franklin D. Roosevelt

An historian and archivist by profession, James Whitehead was a curator at the Franklin Delano Roosevelt Library in Hyde Park. This article is a reprint of one Mr. Whitehead wrote that was published in The Conservationist *(May-June 1977).*

Library in November 1940, the President, presumably, had not been on a real birding trip in years. After three of us on the library staff took him on such a trip, my good friend, Julian P. Boyd, then head of the Princeton University Library, demanded that I write it up for the library's archives. I did so in the form of a letter and it is published here, with short omissions, for the first time.

May 20, 1942
"Dear Julian,
   …the President has always been interested in birds. As a boy he roamed his father's woods in Hyde Park looking at them, and he startled his father by asking for a gun to shoot them. This was no murderous instinct, it seems; rather, it was a scientific one. He wanted to shoot a male and female of each species and mount them himself. This he did, and…the collection (which is fairly extensive) is still in the 'Big House' here.*

   Now, as you know, I am tremendously interested in birds…and I took up with Allen Frost, who works at the library and is the county's outstanding bird authority… Last May I went with him and two other men on their annual census trip, on which they identify as many birds as possible by sound or sight. The trip lasts all day and takes us all over Dutchess County. It always begins before daylight at Thompson's Pond near Stissing Mountain in the northern part of the county.

   Miss Margaret Suckley also works at the library and is a close friend of the President… She is also a close friend of mine and of Mr. Frost. So we had talked of this bird trip together frequently,

---

FDR prepared only a few of the specimens, however, for the work sickened him. Most were prepared by skilled taxidermists. They are on view in the entrance hall of the Roosevelt Mansion at Hyde Park, now under the management of the National Park Service and open to the public. The skins are in storage as part of the collections of the library, except for several used in the "childhood" section of the museum's displays on FDR's life and career. The library, with its extensive museum, is near the mansion and is also open to the public. It is under the management of the National Archives and Records Service—Author's note.

and she had begged to be taken along this year. We consented. In planning the trip, we casually discussed the President's interest in birds, and we vaguely wondered if he still cared for them. Miss Suckley discussed it with him as early as February, I believe, and he expressed keen interest. She asked him if he wanted to go with us, and he said he would love it. So we made our plans.

We invited Ludlow Griscom from Harvard. He is the best field man in the East and a good friend of Mr. Frost. He used to live in Dutchess County, too, and was well known to the President. The other guest was to be Raymond Guernsey, a Poughkeepsie lawyer who was with us last year.…

On Sunday morning, May 10th, at 3:30 Miss Suckley and Mr. Griscom came for me. We shifted to my car, got Mr. Frost and Mr. Guernsey, and drove from Poughkeepsie to the Hyde Park residence. As we drove up to the closed gate a sleepy trooper looked at us questioningly. I told him, "We are to go on the bird trip with the President." Then he gave us a very sick smile…and let us through.

When we got to the house the long black Secret Service car was there and about five S.S. [sic] men. They all looked at us a bit incredulously, too, and I'm sure they thought us all crazy—the President included. But they told us what to do, making sure that my car would not follow the President's directly.

Everybody got out but me, and the first welcome we got was from Fala. He wagged his whole person at everybody, promptly jumped into my car,…and got as close to me as he could—insisting with a wet pink tongue and a little body quivering with excitement that he be allowed to go. But of course he couldn't, and the butler called him away and put him in the house, I think, I was not sure about that, for the door to the "Big House" opened then, and there sat the President in his wheel chair, all ready to go. He had evidently been ready before we got there, and this was only shortly after four o'clock…

Mr. Frost got in the front of the President's car to direct the chauffeur and Miss Suckley and Mr. Griscom in the back with the President. The car moved off, the Secret Service came next, and Mr. Guernsey and I brought up the rear…

"Birding Party" at Thompson's Pond near Pine Plains, to hear the chorus of waking birds, 4:00 a.m., May 10, 1942, (l to r) Raymond Guernsey, Allen Frost, FDR, M. L. Suckley, Ludlow Griscom. FDR PRESIDENTIAL LIBRARY

The sleepy trooper at the gate was burning a flare for us as we went out to keep any other cars from passing us as we left. There were few cars, though, so early in the morning. The President chose the early morning part of the trip to avoid creating attention and also to get back to his weekend guests, the Crown Prince and Crown Princess of Norway, who were probably sound asleep through all this.

It was a horribly damp and cloudy morning…but after we got up country the President had the top of his car put back anyway. Several times we stopped along the way to stay quiet and listen for the night sounds. We heard many whippoorwills, of course, and one or two field birds (various sparrows mainly) chirping every now and then. A catbird sang once.

At Thompson's Pond, a little after five, we stopped on a little road built right through the center of the marsh—reeds and grasses growing thick on both sides. We got out and listened to the early morning chorus of marsh birds—most of us around the President's car. He naturally stayed in it, and so did Miss Suckley. Mr. Griscom stood up to see better, as day came. The Secret Service stood at a respectful distance, all of them bored. They listened kindly, though, as Mr. Frost and Mr. Griscom explained various sounds now and then.

The President spoke in half-whispers at first, as the rest of us did. It was a very awe-inspiring thing to come in the early dawn and hear all these birds filling the silence with their cries. Only as day came did we speak more naturally. The President obviously enjoyed it all very much and asked a number of questions…The President knows little now of birds, I think… But lots of it came back to him… He seemed quite as interested and as confused as Miss Suckley and I at the sounds of Virginia rails, sora rails, American bitterns, marsh wrens, pied-billed grebes, Florida gallinules, and other such things.…

I talked to him very little,…but I stood a couple of feet away from him and heard all that was said. Most of the talk was on birds, but it shifted every now and then…to little anecdotes that he got a great kick out of telling. While we were there he noticed me only twice… One time was when I pointed out a little bird…we had heard but had not seen… The other time was when Mr. Frost and I were telling the party about a silly incident that happened the year before.

Another bird watcher and I thought we heard an owl quite near, and we went in search of it. But the more I heard it the more it sounded like one of our Southern hound dogs; we couldn't find the owl, and actually there came snuffling through the bushes a little brown and black beagle. Not stopping to think that beagles don't make that kind of sound, we accepted the demonstrated fact that he had made it. Only later did we realize it had been an owl all the time.

The President liked the story and promptly remarked, "Evidently the dog had been blowing his beagle at you." At which he laughed, and we all groaned in mock distress. That delighted him, for he evidently enjoys an exaggerated response to puns of that sort— which he himself enjoys to make, simply because they are so bad.

He told two other stories: One was about ducks—I forget what kind—but it is supposedly the most delicious in the world, and the President almost visibly smacked his lips to remember several meals he had made of them. On some trip, he had told Steve Early (his White House Secretary) to shoot him such a duck if he could. Steve did, and on the way back the game warden stopped him and was aghast at seeing two of these ducks. He demanded $25 each. Steve was aghast then and said he didn't know they were protected. The game warden didn't care. Steve then said, "But they are for the President of the United States." The game warden still didn't care. He wanted fifty dollars. In the end Steve had to pay. He bore the duck to the President and told him accusingly what had happened. The President laughed, of course, and enjoyed the ducks in spite of their high cost. He said he had not read the game laws in some time and had not realized that they were no longer to be shot as game. I think he has not had one since.

The other story concerned some Army patrol planes that spotted twenty-one submarines recently near Bermuda. They were all on the surface. In great excitement (We had been in the war for five months at that time, and the entire nation was nervous about German submarines along our east coast) the planes rushed back to report and threw the White House, the Navy Department, and the War Department into a state of nervous anticipation. Out flew the bombers ready to blow them out of the ocean—all Navy bombers. They got out and counted twenty-one whales. The President said, with a great laugh, that the Navy now has even more contempt for the Army's knowledge of the sea and ships.

By this time it was broad daylight, and it had begun to rain. We turned around, went back into a wooded place near the pond, listened to a few forest birds, and then the President had the top of his car put up. He and the people with him proceeded to eat sandwiches and coffee for breakfast (the President had had nothing), and he sent some back to Mr. Guernsey and me—which we refused because we had some of our own.

After this Miss Suckley got us all together around the President's car and took a picture with a little flash camera. She took one, and I took another. The President…seemed to enjoy having the pictures taken.

When I was near him for a moment…he asked if I had ever put a string on a branch and watched the robins play with it—that he had done it as a boy. I had not, of course, and said "no," expressing surprise. He added that they played with it just as kittens would. Of course, even though he is friendly and one forgets his great power, I was more or less tongue-tied in his presence and did not think until later that I should have said—equaling his bad pun—'But Mr. President, I thought only catbirds would do that.'

…After the pictures, he left—bidding us all a very kind goodbye. We were all a little dazed but soon got over it, went on with our observations, and welcomed the sun around nine o'clock. It shone on us all the rest of the day. We identified 108 different species. The President plans to go with us again.…"

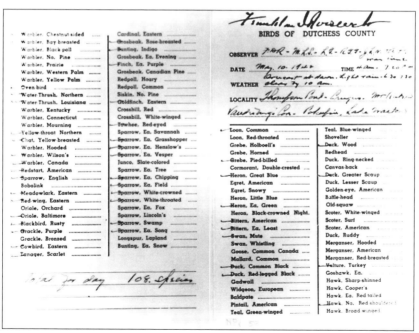

The President's checklist for birds.
FDR PRESIDENTIAL LIBRARY AND *CONSERVATIONIST* MAGAZINE

Gentleman Farmer, 'Hick from Dutchess County'

Franceska Macsali Urbin

Franklin Delano Roosevelt was born a patrician, educated as a lawyer and emerged a master politician. He served as Assistant Secretary of the Navy and was elected to three political offices: the New York State Senate, the Governorship of New York State, and the Presidency of the United States. Even so, he always identified with the farmer. In his heart and mind he was one of them.

Certainly Dutchess County, the part of New York State from which Franklin Roosevelt originated, was predominately a farming area. FDR liked to say, "I am a hick from Dutchess County," or "I am a hayseed and I am proud of it." The estate where he was born and raised could hardly be classified as a typical farm where the owners rose at the crack of dawn to tend crops or feed the chickens. It was a "Gentleman's Farm" where a superintendent oversaw the everyday work of the place and tenant farmers rented acreage from the landlord. Neither Franklin Roosevelt nor his father ever got their hands dirty tilling the soil or milking the cows.

It was James Roosevelt, FDR's father who purchased the estate in 1867. "Springwood" consisted of 110 acres, a 17-room farmhouse and several outbuildings. James Roosevelt had originally intended to raise trotting horses there; however, he gave it up after his favorite horse was killed in a train wreck during shipment to its new owners.

Franceska Macsali Urbin was born and raised in the Hudson Valley. She holds a Bachelor of Arts degree in History from Marist College and a Masters of Science degree from SUNY New Paltz. Ms. Urbin is employed at the Roosevelt-Vanderbilt National Historic Sites as the Supervisory Park Ranger at the homes of Franklin and Eleanor Roosevelt

Franklin was born at Springwood in 1882, and from the time he was able to sit astride a pony he would accompany his father on his daily rounds of the property. Through his father he learned to appreciate the land. From childhood, FDR's "roots" were planted at Springwood and would always remain there. No matter where life took him, Springwood was an integral part of his world.

James Roosevelt died in 1900 when FDR was 18 years old. His property and money were inherited by FDR's mother, Sara Delano Roosevelt. She had been well trained in the business of managing an estate by her own father. Although Franklin hoped he would eventually manage the property, Sara never relinquished control until the day she died in 1941. A letter was written to President Roosevelt in 1938 offering to sell him some prime chickens. FDR's reply was: "Tell Ryan Duffy that I have no chickens of my own and that my mother has special chickens which she does not want to mix with any others."[1]

Over the years Franklin Roosevelt continually attempted to convince his mother to allow him to make changes at Springwood. He felt that they would result in a more cost-effective operation but she was adamant that James Roosevelt's management methods be continued. Sometimes FDR would tease his mother about the costs involved in running the place the "old fashioned way." At breakfast he would ask the guests if they enjoyed the eggs. He would then state that they should be very good indeed because they cost 50 cents each to produce. However, no matter what FDR said, nothing would change. Sara's superintendent, Mr. Plog, said that she did keep careful watch over everything on a daily basis when she was at Springwood. Although FDR could ask Mr. Plog to do things it was understood that ultimately Sara's word was the final one when it came to decisions about Springwood.

FDR became very interested in forestry and planting trees in areas where the soil was depleted and no longer usable for crops. His mother allowed him to experiment in forestry at Springwood and to keep a journal. However, FDR longed to have land of his own to manage. In 1911 he purchased his first piece of property,

Governor Franklin D. Roosevelt driving his car over narrow roads on his 400-acre farm at Hyde Park, N.Y., April 1932. Used with permission. AP/WIDE WORLD PHOTOS

the 194-acre Bennett farm east of Springwood. Finally he had land he could manage. Here he could conduct the forestry experiments in which he was so interested without having to consult with his mother. He also leased a small section of it to his wife, Eleanor, and her friends, Nancy Cook and Marion Dickerman. This part of the property where they would construct a cottage and factory building became known as Val-Kill.

Part of the Bennett farm was rented to Moses Smith. He was actually FDR's first tenant farmer in 1920 and became a very important part of his life over the years. He was FDR's local "sounding board." Roosevelt visited with him on a regular basis and consulted with Smith on the speeches he wanted to deliver. He rationalized that if Moses Smith understood the points he was trying to make, others would as well. Programs he thought about initiating when he was Governor of New York and then President were also discussed with Moses. It was during one of his visits that he shared his concerns about some elderly Hyde Park neighbors who had lost their farm and ended up in the "poor house." Governor Roosevelt said to Smith: "This thing can't go on. I'm going to find some way or some how to put over an old age security so that the poor house in time will actually be done away with."[2] It was the beginning of FDR's plan for a program to assist the elderly that became known as Social Security.

Moses Smith's rental farm, "Woodlawns," consisted of 140 acres. He lived there with his wife and four children. It was rented on a cash basis, not share cropping. Mr. Smith raised corn, strawberries, asparagus and other small crops on his acreage. He also had some 35 dairy cows. According to Smith, FDR never interfered with the running of the farm. Smith did the small repairs on buildings himself and FDR, as landlord, took care of the bigger ones. Sometimes, however, the repairs were a bit slow in getting done as FDR tended to be frugal in money matters. The farmhouse at Woodlawns dated back to the late 1700s; it lacked indoor plumbing and the roof leaked. Until 1926 there was no electricity. When FDR visited the house around 1925 he realized that major repairs were needed. It wasn't until ten years later that the situation was addressed, and only then because Mrs. Smith finally wrote to the President.

> Dear Sir,
> I am sorry to trouble you but… I would like to recall to your mind the period before you were elected Governor when you … were here for a while one afternoon, and upon leaving you noticed the dining room and the kitchen floors, and told me you would give me new flooring. Of course they are worse now, and when the heater was put in the house Mose had to go under the kitchen floor and brace it up, because the weight of the hot water tank made it sag. I wanted him to tell you, but he said that you were too busy; now I feel that it is my duty to tell you the condition of the house …
> When it rains I have to put pails under the leaks in the kitchen and bathroom, and on the north side of the house it beats in and ruins the wallpaper…. So I am asking you to

please roof the house and fix the north side, and to give me
the new floorings which you promised so long ago, also the
new back porch. I certainly would appreciate the heating
system, for we nearly freeze every winter, as it is impossible
to heat the front part of the house with the small fireplaces
there....[3]

President Roosevelt wrote back and said that he would fix the
roof, brace the floor and put in new flooring and make other needed
repairs, but it could not exceed $343. He said that was all he could
afford. This did not include a new heating system. Despite this,
Moses Smith called Franklin Roosevelt "the greatest landlord a man
could have." He continued renting the farm until 1947.

FDR's other tenant farmer was Pete Rohan. In 1937 he
purchased 140 acres of land from Pete's father, Dick, who operated
a dairy farm. Then Roosevelt rented it back to Pete. FDR wanted
to purchase the rest of the farm from Dick Rohan, but he wouldn't
sell it, stating that Roosevelt would have to wait "until I die." It was
on part of the Rohan tract that FDR would build Top Cottage, the
Dutch colonial style house that he planned to use as a retreat when
he retired from the Presidency.

Over the years FDR acquired many other small pieces of land.
He purchased the Tompkins farm and rented the house to Nellie
Johannessen. He also planted trees on the land. He bought tracts
of land from the Archibald Rogers estate and from his next door
neighbor, the Newbolds. On one piece of property, he had a barn
converted to a two-family house and a wagon shed into three
apartments. These were rented to Hyde Park families for $15 to $20
a month. Although FDR initially used his mother's superintendent
for his land, in 1939 he hired his own superintendent, Russell
Linaka, to oversee his property.

Eventually the entire Roosevelt property would consist of 1600
acres of land. This included 800 acres of native wood, 400 acres
of tree plantations and 400 in orchards, pastures, tilled fields and
abandoned homes. Although it was classified as Roosevelt land in
general, in reality it was divided into "his" (Franklin's) and "hers"

(Sara's). FDR also had a network of roads built on the estate. According to Frank Draiss, who helped construct them, Roosevelt wanted them "just so he could drive around and look over the woods and renew the scenes of his childhood when he used to ride around on those bridal paths in the old days." [4]

Franklin Roosevelt would use his land for two purposes, forestry experiments and rent. He didn't work the land himself. Like his father, FDR was a gentleman farmer. Although he didn't actually sow or plough or reap, he felt close to the land and a kinship with the farmer. He always said he was proud to be one.

NOTES

1. The President's Personal Papers 1G—Hyde Park—1938, Franklin Delano Roosevelt Library

2. Interview with Moses Smith by George Palmer, National Park Service, Home of Franklin D. Roosevelt Historic Site, January 1948.

3. Ward, Geoffrey, *A First Class Temperament, The Emergence of Franklin Roosevelt*, New York, NY, Harper and Row Publishers, 1989, p. 762

4. Interview with Frank Draiss by George Palmer, National Park Service, Home of Franklin D. Roosevelt National Historic Site, January 1952

The Forest Plantations at Hyde Park

Thomas W. Patton

Franklin and Eleanor Roosevelt toured the historic forests of Europe during their honeymoon. Writing home to his mother, Sara, FDR described the beauty of the German forests: "…the mist rising after the soaking of the last few days…was lovely and showed most of the Black Forests… The moisture on all the trees and undergrowth and the bright sun made it very picturesque."[1] After visiting an opulent country estate in England, he informed Sara that his plans for their Hyde Park estate, "now include not only a new house, but new farms, cattle, trees, etc"[2] With his election to the New York State Senate from Hyde Park in 1910, FDR was able to start implementing these plans by taking a more active role in the operation of Springwood. However, Sara would never completely relinquish control of the estate to her son and the property remained in her name until she died in 1941.

Sara was primarily interested in the traditional pleasantries of a country estate: the dairy farm with its Alderney cattle, which produced such rich milk, the orchards, vegetable and flower gardens. Her rose garden, where Franklin and Eleanor are buried was her favorite. After her husband, James, had died in 1900, Sara wished:

Thomas W. Patton grew up in Hyde Park, New York and this background nurtured his interest in FDR and later, FDR's promotion of forestry. He received his Ph.D. in History at New York University and taught history at Long Beach High School on Long Island. Patton maintains his roots in Dutchess County through historical research and writing and, quite literally, through the development of his own tree plantations. This article is reprinted from the Dutchess County Historical Society 1985 Year Book.

"...to run it just as her husband had. It was to be a gentleman's country place, not a farm run for profit...." However, according to Eleanor, "my husband (FDR) should take over the wooded part of the place."[3]

While Sara tended to the farm and gardens, Franklin managed the woods and worked to convert the farm to the production of trees. Forestry, rather than the traditional forms of Hudson Valley agriculture, was Roosevelt's primary interest. FDR first directed his farm crew to clear overgrown farmland for tree planting in 1911 and the following year he placed his first order for seedlings with the New York State Conservation Commission. That year he ordered 5,000 White Pine seedlings and Scotch Pine, Red Pine and Norway Spruce seedlings in lots of 1,000. Except for the five years (1919-1923), during which Franklin Roosevelt was serving in Washington and then recuperating from polio, FDR ordered trees every year until his death. Nearly one half million trees were obtained, most of which came from the State of New York.

When Franklin and Eleanor Roosevelt viewed the famous forests of Europe they were observing a centuried tradition of forestry. Ehrufurth, Germany first developed a forest management plan in 1359. When America was settled forestry seemed to be unnecessary. This nation was so blessed with forests that, for nearly 300 years after the start of European settlement, trees were considered as much a curse as a blessing. Trees hindered development and forests were thought to be the dwelling place of evil. Nearly one half of America's land surface was forested and the eastern portion of the continent was almost completely covered by trees. Forest soils and trees were the nation's most extensive natural resources.

As the American land rush reached the Pacific and the end of the horn of plenty, a few Americans started to question the nation's land and forest policy. Leading the debate for more scientific resource management was a small group of naturalist writers and scientists. The most important study of nature history during this period, *Man and Nature*, written by George Perkins Marsh, was published in 1864. *Man and Nature* set forth the enduring theme that natural resources and man are inextricably interrelated. If one resource, to use Marsh's phrase, "The Woods," was damaged or destroyed, all other resources and mankind suffered. To illustrate, Marsh described how thriving areas of China, Europe and North Africa became destitute, environmentally and economically, after the forest growth was removed. The example of the results of forest devastation in China was frequently cited by early conservationists. When FDR invited Gifford Pinchot to address the Forest, Fish and Game Committee of the State Senate in 1912, Pinchot showed a lantern slide of a forested valley in China and a second slide showing the same valley after it had been deforested. The environmental and human devastation illustrated in the second slide made a lasting impression on Franklin Roosevelt.[4]

While forest devastation continued at a hectic pace, writers focused on this destruction as the major conservation problem. An upstate physician, Franklin Benjamin Hough, convinced the Federal government in 1878 to study forest conditions. *The Report Upon Forestry* documented forest destruction but also noted that a fledgling tree planting program had been started in the plains states where trees had always been valued. Nebraska, a leader, first celebrated Arbor Day in 1872.

During the decade that FDR was born, a movement developed to pressure the United States Government to retain undistributed forested areas of the western domain. The president was authorized to establish a forest reserve in 1891 and President Harrison withdrew thirteen million acres to create the first national forest.

The history of forest destruction and forestry in New York illustrated that of the other eastern states. Trees were originally considered to be a hindrance and wantonly burnt, then lumbered as the state became the nation's largest timber producer. By the Civil War the supply of first-growth trees was being exhausted and production had started a steady decline. New York led the nation in lumber production in 1850, was second in 1860, fourth in 1890, seventeenth in 1900 and twenty-second in 1910.[5] Interrelated with the history of forestry in New York is the history of conventional agriculture. As the land was tilled the forests were destroyed. As conventional agriculture was abandoned, the forests started regenerating. With the opening of free and inexpensive fertile land in the West, which New York State facilitated by building the Erie Canal, New York's farmers were tilling less fertile land each year and found it increasingly difficult to compete against western farmers in all but perishable farm products. Before the Civil War, hill farms were being abandoned in New York and from 1880-1917 approximately 40,000 acres a year were being deserted.[6] Dutchess County reached its maximum level of deforestation in 1890.

Stimulated by the early deforestation and subsequent abandonment of its farmland, New York was a leader in state forestry efforts. A general forestry law, passed in 1885, was described as: "The first comprehensive forest administration law in the United States"[7] created the Adirondack and Catskill forest preserves, established a forest commission and modernized fire protection. Five years later the "forever wild" requirement for the forest preserves, was added to the State Constitution. New York was also a leader of the "tree-planting crusade,"[8] starting financial support for tree planting in 1869 when it provided for an abatement of the highway tax if a landowner planted trees by the side of a public road. The Forest, Fish and Game Commission, predecessor to the Department of Environmental Conservation, started raising seedlings for distribution to private landowners in 1902. By 1910 New York surpassed all other states and the Federal government in the production of seedlings. Its Saratoga Springs nursery was one of the largest nurseries in the world, producing nearly three million trees a year.[9]

As the tree-planting crusade gained momentum early in the twentieth century the owners of several large estates in Dutchess County started reforesting their land. East of Hyde Park, in Millbrook, Charles F. Dietrich had transformed his farm into a manor worthy of an English lord. A high fence kept the stocked game in and unwelcome villagers out. More significantly in the history of forestry, in 1894 Dietrich started planting conifer seedlings which he imported from Germany. As did the Hyde Park estate owners, including the Roosevelts, Dietrich planted White Pines to shield his property from the highway, but he also planted stands of Norway Spruce, Scotch Pine and European Larch.[10] Writing in 1923, A.B. Recknagle, a Cornell forestry specialist, described one of Dietrich's stands of Norway Spruce as being "the best for Norway Spruce in the State."[11] Also in Millbrook, Samuel and Oakleigh Thorne established model plantations in the first decade of the century. Oakleigh Thorne planted White Pine, Red Pine and White Oak. Cooperating with the United States Forest Service, Samuel Thorne established a plantation of Red Oak.[12]

Frederick W. Vanderbilt, the brother of George W. Vanderbilt who, under the direction of Gifford Pinchot, developed his North Carolina Estate, "Biltmore," into an American model of scientific forestry, bought the Bard-Hosack estate just north of the village of Hyde Park in 1895. John Bard (1716-1799) and his son Samuel (1742-1821) were among America's notable early physicians. The Tory and slave holding Bards were also agricultural experimenters. They imported Merino sheep to improve local stock, used clover and gyspum to improve their soil[13] and planted specimen trees so that eventually their estate took on the "character of an arboretum."[14] David Hosack, a medical partner of Samuel Bard, owned the property from 1828 to 1835. He carried on the horticultural effort of the Bards and employed Andre Parmetier, a Belgian landscape gardener to design the paths, road and vistas of the estate, which:

> …comprised 700 acres and in its day was unsurpassed for its orchards and flower and vegetable gardens. Dr. Hosack is well known in Europe, and through acquaintances there introduced many new fruits from European orchards which eventually came into the hands of fruit growers in the Hudson River Valley.[15]

Frederick Vanderbilt continued the ornamental plantings on the estate. He planted White Pines to shield the estate from the

---

Opposite: Map of plantations on the Estate of Governor Franklin D. Roosevelt.
FDR PRESIDENTIAL LIBRARY

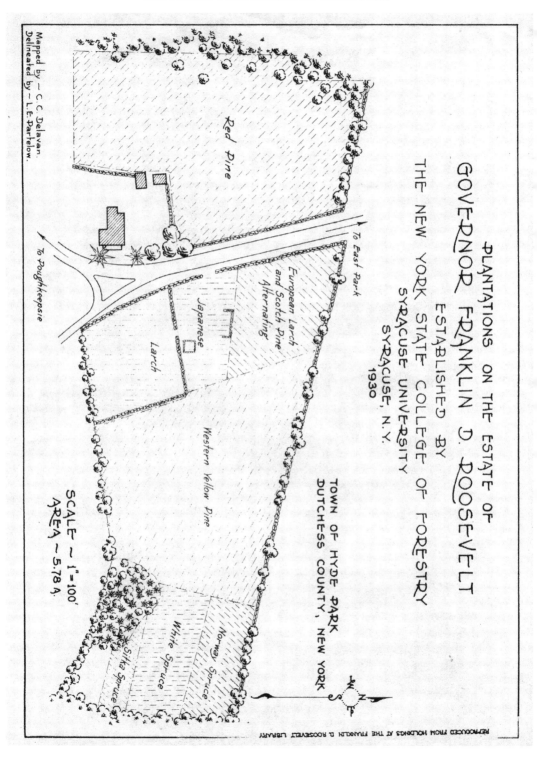

PLANTATIONS ON THE ESTATE OF
GOVERNOR FRANKLIN D. ROOSEVELT
ESTABLISHED BY
THE NEW YORK STATE COLLEGE OF FORESTRY
SYRACUSE UNIVERSITY
SYRACUSE, N.Y.
1930

TOWN OF HYDE PARK
DUTCHESS COUNTY, NEW YORK

Red Pine

European Larch
and Scotch Pine
Alternating

Japanese
Larch

Western Yellow Pine

Norway Spruce

White Spruce

Sitka Spruce

To East Park

To Poughkeepsie

Mapped by ~ C. C. Delavan.
Delineated by ~ L.E. Parlelow.

SCALE ~ 1"=100'
AREA ~ 5.78 A.

Post Road and several White Pine plantations on the farmland to the east.

"Crumwold Farms," the estate of Archibald Rogers, lay between the Vanderbilt and Roosevelt properties. Unlike the Vanderbilts, whom the Roosevelts judged to be too pretentious, the members of the Rogers family were close friends with the Roosevelts. Archibald Rogers had helped Theodore Roosevelt found the Boone and Crockett Club and FDR's first schooling took place in the Rogers' home. Contrasting Frederick Vanderbilt, Archibald Rogers emphasized practical forestry. Forestry, while it had ornamental or aesthetic value, was primarily aimed toward measurable financial and ecological returns. Starting in the 1890's Rogers undertook to improve the forest stock through improvement cutting and in 1905 he entered into a "cooperative agreement" with the United States Forest Service, which prepared, "A Working Plan for the Woodland on Crumwold Farms, the Estate of Archibald Rogers, Hyde Park-on-Hudson." The same year Rogers started one of New York's first tree nurseries.[16]

J. Nelson Spaeth of the Department of Forestry at Cornell did a twenty-year follow-up study of Roger's forest in 1925. Describing it as an "absolute forest land" of the "sprout hardwood type of the Central Hardwood Region,"[17] he examined the growth of the 43 compartments the Forest Service had delineated in 1905. Spaeth concluded that Rogers' forestry operation was a success with the growth of the hardwoods and White Pines occurring at an acceptable rate.[18]

As a careful observer of Dutchess County it is likely that Franklin Roosevelt would have known about the forestry efforts of his fellow estate owners. He certainly followed Rogers' forestry work, describing him in 1915 as being "really expert in practical forestry."[19] By that date the future president had started the educational process to earn that description for himself.

Franklin Roosevelt felt strongly about the land between the Roosevelt home and the Hudson River. Visible below the home were the woods and fields he had first explored as a youth. When he started his forestry plantings in 1912 perhaps as much as one half of this land was open, being used for pasture or possibly tilled crops. Growing on a series of stone outcroppings directly below the home is a pocket of oaks and hemlocks which Roosevelt and consulting foresters considered to be virgin first-growth trees. This section of the estate was carefully preserved in accordance with the directions of a consulting forester who cautioned Roosevelt: "The stand should remain untouched. Do not remove even dead trees. Do not build new roads. Thus it will be preserved just as nature has treated it."[20] After the President's death, the National Park Service has continued to carefully protect these woods.

Interspersed through the forest below the home are pockets of trees, which Roosevelt planted on the worn out farmland. These plantings of Red Pine, Scotch Pine, White Pine, Norway Spruce and Tulip Poplar (Liriodendron tulipifera), which was FDR's favorite tree, have not been maintained.

Several of Franklin Roosevelt's first forest plantings line the historic gravel road that winds its way from the river up to the home. FDR drove foreign dignitaries up this road from the family's railroad siding and on April 14, 1945 a horse-drawn caisson followed the same path to the rose garden for the President's burial. Just below the rose garden and the crest of the hill, and to the right of the road, is a stand of White Pine that was planted in 1915 and pruned in 1930. Continuing down the road, on the right, past the turnoff to the servants' quarters, are plantings of Tulip Poplar made in 1917 and 1928. While these trees have been overgrown with competitors and have had a low survival rate, some excellent poplars remain with one tree measuring over 100 feet in height.[21] To the left of the road and at the edge of the field directly below the home is a small stand of Norway Spruce that may have been planted the first year that FDR started planting trees.

The tall and graceful American Chestnut (Castanea dentatla, Marsh.), which was able to thrive in a wide variety of soil conditions, had been the dominant forest tree of Dutchess County since before the Dutch arrived. Its dense wood, high in tannic acid and therefore decay-resistant, was highly valued for fencing, crossties, telegraph poles, construction lumber and furniture wood. But it was for its fall crop of sweet and very edible nuts, which were superior to the small and tartish Oriental varieties that have replaced them, that the American Chestnut is remembered. For the River Families, the gathering of chestnuts was a favored activity, which gave added purpose to fall walks through the resplendent Hudson Valley forests. James Roosevelt had directed young Franklin to favored trees on the family estate and in his turn, FDR enjoyed showing the trees to his children while enlisting them in the harvest.

The chestnut blight, which was caused by the fungus Endothia paransitia, was first identified in New Bronx, New York in 1904. The disease quickly spread northward, first reaching Hyde Park about 1915. The devastation of the fungus is as insidious as it is complete. As the disease travels through a forest some parts of individual trees and some entire trees appear to be immune for several years. Sprouts, which grow from diseased trunks often vigorously, reach a height of twenty or more feet before finally succumbing to the disease. This uneven destruction led foresters and woodlot owners to report numerous examples of individual trees, which appeared to be immune from the blight. As reported by *The New York Times* on October 4, 1938, Franklin Roosevelt was a victim of this false hope:

> Hyde Park, N.Y. (Oct. 2)—A chance discovery by President Roosevelt on his Dutchess Hill forestation project today may mean that the all but extinct chestnut tree, devastated by a mysterious blight several years ago, may be coming back.[22]

Later that year and in a more scientific manner, FDR initiated the planting of various varieties of Oriental Chestnuts to test their adaptability and productivity. Professor Nelson Brown of the College of Forestry at Syracuse suggested the chestnut plantings to Roosevelt and convinced the Bureau of Plant Industry of the Department of Agriculture that it was appropriate to supply the

President with planting stock. The Department of Agriculture had distributed more than 200,000 chestnut seedlings to various Federal, state and private projects in its search for a replacement for the American Chestnut.[23] FDR enthusiastically agreed with Brown's suggestion: "I shall be delighted to try the experiment of the Asiatic Chestnuts next spring."[24]

A total of 350 Japanese Chestnut (Castanean crenata) and Chinese Chestnut (Castanea mollissima) seedlings, of different strains were planted by Roosevelt workers in a pasture FDR had purchased from the Morgan family in 1936. Described as the "northwest Newbold lot," it is located in the large woods west of "Bellefield," the Newbold-Morgan home, which is now occupied by the National Park Service. The seedlings were planted in accordance with the requirements of the Department of Plant Industry and were identified by tree markers. Initially, the seedlings were healthy, with 95% of the 1938 plantings surviving the first year, which was unusually dry, and the plantation reached a height of two to six feet by 1942 with a 90% survival rate. However in 1945, Nelson Brown reported that the Oriental Chestnuts were forming numerous shoots and were in need of pruning.[25]

It appears that all of the experimental chestnuts have died. Numerous searches by the author and personnel of the National Park Service have failed to discover any surviving specimens. Since they were planted in a scientific manner, which included a site map, the discovery of even a few surviving trees would be valuable to determine the outcome of one of Franklin Roosevelt's forestry experiments.

Through a series of land purchases, which began in 1911 and continued until 1938, FDR doubled the size of the Roosevelt property to a total of nearly 1,600 acres. With the exception of the purchase of the Morgan lot, these purchases extended the estate to the east, straddling Route 9-G. In 1925 Eleanor Roosevelt with two of her friends, had a stone cottage built, which she named "Val-Kill," on a gentle rise facing the tranquil Fallkill Creek and a large open pasture to the west. This property is accessible by a well-marked driveway just north of the 9-G/Creek Road triangle.

It is likely that the land on this part of the estate, the majority of which is gently undulating with loose, well-drained soil, "Dutchess Stony loam and Merrimac gravelly loam,"[26] had been farmed since the American Revolution. While it was originally productive, by the time FDR acquired the land the soil was depleted. Roosevelt commented: "I can lime it, cross-plough it, manure it and treat it with every art known to science, but it has just plain run out." [27] Facing this realization FDR searched for an alternative crop with which to use the land productively. Following the example of other Dutchess County estate owners and continuing his early plantings surrounding the home, Roosevelt started planting trees on his Val-Kill farmland. Plantings were made in this area every spring until after the President's death when, for a few years, Elliott Roosevelt took over management of the Val-Kill property. During the latter thirties and in the forties FDR increasingly turned his attention to the production of Christmas trees and as many as 50,000 seedlings were planted annually.

There are two notable forestry plantations in the immediate area of Mrs. Roosevelt's cottage. The far superior one is the White Pine plantation north of the cottage. This plantation, which was a favorite of Eleanor Roosevelt, grows across the brook from the furniture factory on the northern and easterly edges of the pond. On clear days the pines are framed against the blue sky and in the late summer and early fall, purple loosestrife, which Mrs. Roosevelt regarded highly as her "purple weed,"[28] provided a colorful prelude to the woods. The plantation, which was probably planted in 1934 or '35, is generally free of competing trees as well as any major insect or disease infestation. Some twenty years after the date of planting,[29] the treetops had spread enough to almost totally shade the forest floor. Here the heavy carpet of pine needles is pierced by a scattering spice bush (Lindera benzoin) and a variety of ferns.

A natural resources inventory completed for the National Park Service in 1979 suggested that this plantation could be improved through thinning:

With proper thinning and removal of dead and declining stems, this area could be developed into a show place reminiscent of White Pine stands that used to dominate many sites in the northeastern United States. Past growth rates and prevalence of the White Pine-Northern Red Oak-White Ash forest type in the Dutchess County region adjacent to Val-Kill, indicate the site and climatic conditions in this area are suitable to White Pine.[30]

One can speculate about whether Franklin Roosevelt, who emphasized the practical returns of managed forests, or Eleanor Roosevelt, who perhaps had a more aesthetic view of nature, would have agreed on the proposed rehabilitation of the White Pine plantation.

Contrasting the healthy state of growth of the White Pine planting is the condition of the Scotch Pine and arborvitae (Northern White-Cedar) plantation south of the Val-Kill cottage. This small plantation is visible through the natural growth hardwoods and brush in the low area just south of the cottage. It was probably planted in 1929, which was just before the foresters from the College of Forestry at Syracuse started making regular visits to the Roosevelt Estate. The poor conditions of this planting illustrate the results of poor variety-site location, insect damage and a lack of maintenance. It is likely that most of the crooked and forked trunks of the Scotch Pines were caused by the European Pine shoot moth (Rahyacionia boilina).[31] The arborvitae which were planted to the south of the Scotch Pine have been overgrown by native hardwoods, particularly the moisture-loving Red Maple. This planting is an unfortunate example of what happened so frequently in New York State when the wrong type of tree was introduced on a poor forest site.

Governor Roosevelt met with a delegation from the College of Forestry at Syracuse who came to Albany in 1929 to lobby for a new science building. During the meeting the Governor expressed his interest in forestry, that he "… wanted to see it expand and develop into its proper place in the economic and social development of the state and country,"[32] and he invited one of the Syracuse foresters to visit Hyde Park to consult with him on his forestry plantings. Later that year, Nelson C. Brown, Professor of Forest Utilization, visited Hyde Park. The following January, Roosevelt announced an appropriation for the Syracuse building.

Brown had come to the College of Forestry as one of the original faculty members in 1912 after graduating from the Yale Forestry School and working for private lumber companies and the U.S. Forest Service. Through his extensive writings, over 200 articles and a dozen books which explained and popularized forestry with a minimum of technical language, his excellent speaking ability and affable personality, Brown promoted forestry—the College of Forestry—and himself. Professor Brown believed that undue emphasis was placed on laboratory-microscope work and that, instead, the natural sciences should emphasize fieldwork. Throughout the school year Brown and his students visited forestry operations in upstate New York and each summer he conducted an extensive tour of southern forests.

Professor Brown visited Hyde Park every year until 1947, advising the Roosevelts on their forestry operation. Each winter he would formulate a planting program for the following spring; during world War II when the demand and price for lumber were high, Brown marked the Roosevelt hardwoods to be cut, drew up the necessary contracts, secured a buyer, supervised the cutting and forest cleanup and saw to it that the President got paid. Brown was never paid for his services or expenses and when he sent President Roosevelt several "I am available" letters,[33] he had to satisfy himself with an informal summer assignment observing the operation of the Civilian Conservation Corps in the western states. Other Syracuse foresters who visited Hyde Park were Svend Heiberg, a forest soil specialist, Ray Bower, who supervised plantings, and C.C. Delavan who mapped some of the Roosevelt-Syracuse plantings. A 1931 graduate of the College of Forestry who also contributed to managed forestry on the Roosevelt Estate was Irving Isenberg who lived with the Roosevelts the summer he graduated while he prepared "A Management Plan For Kromelbooge Woods At Hyde Park, N.Y., for the period 1931-1941."

While they were formulating the planting program for 1930, Roosevelt and Brown, who was acting dean, agreed that the College and the governor would informally cooperate in establishing some experimental and demonstration plantations on the Roosevelt Estate. FDR had unsuccessfully attempted to reach a similar agreement with the New York State Conservation Commission in 1924. Dean Brown wrote to FDR in the spring of 1930 outlining the objectives and operation of the Roosevelt-Syracuse plantings:

> The plantations along the highway 9-G are intended as purely demonstration forests. The others are intended as experimental plantations. Very careful records will be kept of spacing, types of soil, character and size of trees used, etc., which will give us the basis of data which will guide us in drawing conclusions as to results in the years to come. It is intended to follow up these initial plantings with further experiments next year—…with your permission we should like to use this as one of our experimental stations. This can be done without any definite commitment by you except to continue the excellent plan of management which you have apparently been following in the past.
>
> It will be intended to improve the woods and to handle it as a commercial forestry operation. We have no experimental operations in the Hudson Valley and your tract offers an excellent opportunity for some cooperative experiments not only in reforestation but in woodlot management.
>
> …we should like very much to announce these cooperative experiments if it is agreeable.[34]

The largest remaining stand from the Roosevelt-Syracuse planting effort, one which N.C. Brown ironically described as "purely demonstration," is located west of 9-G where it intersects with Creek Road. This "demonstration" planting of Red Pine has not been maintained. It is diseased, overgrown with competitors, unthinned, unpruned, and littered with trees that have blown down. Although it was a popular reforestation tree in the 1930s, the selection of Red Pine is questionable. It is highly susceptible to disease and wind damage while its main use is for wood pulp that does not have a local market. Fifty years after its planting, this stand is a demonstration of poor forestry.

An area that Franklin Roosevelt called "Tamarack Swamp" on the Tompkins farm which he purchased in 1925, provided Roosevelt and the Syracuse foresters with a challenge in historical and ecological investigation and forest planting. "Tamarack Swamp" is located in the fork formed by Route 9-G and Creek Road and extends southward to where the Roosevelt property ended at what is now Judy Terrace.

President Roosevelt was intrigued by the historical and ecological implications of the local name of the overgrown swamp since the Tamarack tree was not native to Dutchess County during his lifetime. The Tamarack tree did, however, grow in the higher elevations of the Catskill and Pennsylvania mountains to the west. Professor Brown related the story that FDR had hunted in the swamp as a boy and that he had unearthed some old stumps which were identified as Tamarack. Roosevelt never recorded this story but he was interested in the swamp and the questions which it posed:

> This occurrence of Tamarack interested him very much and he often spoke of it. He also wondered about the extent to which Tamarack was found in the Hudson Valley, how it happened to grow in this particular swamp, what the early settlers used it for and why it had disappeared. This study of tree ecology is evidence of his wide interests, his fertile mind and willingness to investigate some matters that may not be of any current economic importance but was of great interest from a biological and historic viewpoint.[35]

FDR was also challenged by the difficulty of upgrading the trees which were growing in the wet area; "…a very dense stand of Red Maple, some Elm, Popple and Swamp White Oak."[36] In 1931 he had the swamp cleared, drained and replanted with more valuable trees. This work was performed under the direction of Ray Bower of the College of Forestry. When the ditches were dug, Bower noted that the humus layer was "…almost comparable to the peat bogs of Ireland."[37] Arborvitae, Tulip Poplar, Norway Spruce, White Pine, European Larch and Beech were planted on the drained land. Less than 10% of the White Pine, Poplar, Norway Spruce and Larch are surviving today. All the surviving trees are clustered on the higher ground. Apparently they were never thinned and are severely stunted. A volunteer growth of Red Maple has replaced most of the plantation seedlings. A decade after the President's death sections of the swamp were cleared for houses and a trailer park.

FDR considered this replanting effort to be a failure:

> It is the one failure that we have made. We have tried three different plantings on it, but the damned thing won't grow. However, the State Forestry people are going to try it with these Larches.[38]

Attractive stands and individual trees can be seen in the yards of homes which were built after World War II on former Roosevelt property along Creek and Roosevelt Roads. The conifers on both sides of Creek Road south from 9-G were planted by Roosevelt crews in the thirties and early forties. Beginning at its terminus with Lawrence Road east of 9-G and continuing about one half mile, Roosevelt Road transects what was Roosevelt property. On both sides of the road, conifers which were primarily intended by Franklin Roosevelt to become Christmas trees, are gracing the yards of the homes. Ironically, since most of the trees were removed and many of those that were left have been subject to blow-down, those that remain have had the proper space to grow and are specimen trees.

Two aspects of FDR's forestry efforts, the sale of improved hardwoods during World War II and the sale of Christmas trees, returned some money. No financial return was derived from the conifers which Roosevelt planted for timber production. Roosevelt's return did not equal his investment in land, labor and the cost of the seedlings, but he expected that his efforts would produce an increased return in the future. Two year after his death, Mrs. Roosevelt wrote:

> The results of the years during which my husband bought woodland and planted trees are now beginning to show. While trees are never spectacularly profitable, they certainly are an interesting one, and I think ours should begin now to produce some more adequate returns.[39]

Most of the Roosevelt property was sold during the decade following FDR's death. With the exception of the harvesting of hardwoods in the area between Routes 9 and 9-G and the maintenance efforts of the National Park Service, forestry has stopped on Roosevelt property.

With the continued decline of dairying and most other traditional forms of agriculture in Dutchess County and the consequent increase in the availability of land for growing trees which are regenerating naturally, landowners might consider plantation trees and woodlot improvement as a source of income. Woodlot owners and owners of idle open land might imitate FDR and derive revenue from the sale of hardwoods from an improved woodlot or by raising Christmas trees. If the land is already owned and the tree-grower does not compute the initial land cost as an expense, a "profit" might ensue.

As governor and president, Franklin Roosevelt applied the knowledge of land use and forestry which he learned through his forestry efforts at Hyde Park. New York's forestry program under Roosevelt was "the largest and most constructive yet adopted by any state."[40] FDR successfully campaigned for, and then implemented, the Hewitt Amendment to the State Constitution which funded the purchase and reforestation of neglected land. He established a program which placed 10,000 unemployed men to work in New York's forests. Praising Governor Roosevelt's forestry record, *The Journal of Forestry* commented: "Franklin D. Roosevelt has made full use of his home forestry experiments and experiences."[41]

Franklin Roosevelt did more to promote forestry than any other president. He expanded the national forests as his cousin Teddy had done and he also was responsible for the largest tree planting effort in American history. Through the Civilian Conservation Corps, he focused national attention on conservation. When the C.C.C. was being organized, FDR sketched an organization chart for the Corps, to which he added: "I want personally to check on the location scope etc. of the camps, size work to be done etc. FDR" [sic] This was a pledge he would expertly keep based on his experiences as a Dutchess County "tree grower."

NOTES

[1] FDR to Sara Roosevelt, August 7, 1905, *Personal Letters of Franklin D. Roosevelt*, Vol. II, Elliott Roosevelt, ed. New York: Duell, Sloan and Pearch, pp.57-8.

[2] Joseph P. Lash, *Eleanor and Franklin*, New York, Norton, 1971, p. 150.

[3] Eleanor Roosevelt, "My Day," April 26, 1945.

[4] Franklin D. Roosevelt, Address at Lake Placid, New York, September 14, 1935, *Franklin D. Roosevelt and Conservation*, Vol. I, Edgar B. Nixon, ed., Hyde Park: Franklin D. Roosevelt Library, 1957, p. 430.

[5] A.B.Recknagel, *The Forests of New York State*, New York, Macmillan, 1923, p.28.

[6] Ibid., p.40.

[7] Ibid.

[8] Henry Clepper, *Professional Forestry in the United States* (Baltimore: Johns Hopkins, 1971, p. 216.

[9] Andrew D. Rogers, *Bernhard E. Fernow: A Story of North American Forestry*, Princeton, Princeton University Press, 1951, p. 336.

[10] B. H. Paul, "Reforesting Methods and Results of Forest Planting in New York State," Bulletin 374, Cornell University, 1916, p. 677.

[11] Recknagel, *Forests of New York*, p. 90.

[12] Paul, "Reforestating Methods," p. 677.

[13] Olin Dows, "Franklin Roosevelt at Hyde Park," New York, *American Artists*, 1949, pp. 138-9.

[14] Franklin D. Roosevelt to Rev. M.J. Devine, Aug., 8, 1939, Franklin Delano Roosevelt Library (hereafter FDRL), President's Personal File, 128.

[15] Roland Van Zandt, *Chronicles of the Hudson: Three Centuries of Traveler's Accounts*, New Brunswick, Rutgers, 1971, 335.

[16] Gurth Whipple, *A History of a half a century of the Conservation of Natural Resources of the Empire State, 1885-1935*, Albany, Lyon, 1935, p. 89.

[17] J. Nelson Spaeth, "Twenty Years of Growth of a Sprout Hardwood Forest in

New York: A Study of the Effects of Intermediate and Reproduction Cuttings." Bulletin 465, Cornell University, 1928, p. 4.

[18] Ibid., pp. 47-8.

[19] Franklin Roosevelt to Franklin Moon, *Roosevelt and Conservation*, Vol. I, p. 35.

[20] Irving Isenberg, "Management Plan for Kromebooge Woods at Hyde Park, New York, for the period 1931-1941." 1931, Family, Farm and Personal Business, FDRL, p.4.

[21] Ann Lewis, "Vegetation Resource Inventory for the Home of Franklin D. Roosevelt National Historic Site," 1983, p. 27.

[22] *The New York Times*, October 4, 1938, p. 27.

[23] *Forest Leaves*, XXVII, No. 1., Jan., 1938, p. 13.

[24] Franklin Roosevelt to Nelson C. Brown, June 29, 1937, President's Personal File, FDRL, 38.

[25] Nelson C. Brown, "Planting Report, 1945," Family, Farm and Personal Business, FDRL.

[26] "Soil Map of Dutchess County, New York," United States Department of Agriculture, 1905.

[27] Franklin Roosevelt, April 14, 1931, *Roosevelt and Conservation*, Vol. II, p. 85.

[28] Eleanor Roosevelt, "My Day," August 1, 1947.

[29] "Natural Resources Inventory at Eleanor Roosevelt National Historic Site, Hyde Park, New York," Pandullo Quirk Associates, 1979, p, 29.

[30] Ibid., p. 30.

[31] Ibid., p. 32.

[32] Nelson C. Brown, "Reminiscences of F.D.R.," N.C. Brown Papers, FDRL, p. 11.

[33] Nelson C. Brown to Franklin Roosevelt, December 28, 1932 and March 28, 1933, N.C. Brown Papers, FDRL.

[34] Nelson C. Brown to Franklin Roosevelt, April 4, 1930, Farm, Business and Personal Affairs, Box 74, FDRL.

[35] Nelson C. Brown, "Reminiscences," p. 15.

[36] Ibid., p. 16.

[37] Ray F. Bower, "Governor Roosevelt's Forest," *American Forests*, May 1, 1931, p. 274.

[38] Franklin Roosevelt, Press Conference, July 4, 1936.

[39] Eleanor Roosevelt, "My Day," June 5, 1947.

[40] *Journal of Forestry*, XXX, No. 1, January 1932, p. 2.

[41] Ibid.

Epilogue: On the 60th Anniversary of the President's Death

Sarah Olson

A year to the day after his death Franklin Roosevelt's home opened to the public. April 12, 1946 was a cold and gray spring day with just a few tulips poking up near the President's grave. President Truman traveled to Hyde Park to participate in the ceremony. He stopped first to lay a wreath at his former boss' grave; then he visited with Mrs. Roosevelt inside the home before they joined the many distinguished guests on the front porch. Eleanor Roosevelt had FDR's beloved Fala in tow. Then-Secretary of the Interior, Julius Krug, accepted the home on behalf of the American people from Mrs. Roosevelt. Marian Anderson sang the national anthem.

Some 700 political leaders, diplomats and other notables attended, including nearly all of FDR's former administration, members of the United Nations Security Council, and representatives from 23 foreign nations. On the great lawn stretching from the house to the Albany Post Road were 5,000 others, mainly residents of Hyde Park and Dutchess County who felt a special kinship to their neighbor, FDR. A school holiday was declared so that local children could witness the historic event and schoolgirls worked side by side with their mothers in a canteen tent set up to benefit the Red Cross.[1]

The turnout for the dedication of a president's home was

Sarah Olson has been engaged in preserving and managing cultural properties for the National Park Service for over twenty-five years. She is the superintendent of three National Historic Sites in Hyde Park, New York: the home of Franklin D. Roosevelt, which includes Top Cottage; Eleanor Roosevelt's Val-Kill; and the Vanderbilt Mansion.

unprecedented, as was FDR's decision to set aside his home for the nation. His work with Congress, begun in 1939, that resulted in the establishment of the Home of Franklin D. Roosevelt National Historic Site marked the first time a serving-president donated his home to the people of the United States and set a precedent for future presidents.

In her comments that day Eleanor Roosevelt said one of her husband's considerations in donating his home was that he thought quite a few people would be interested in seeing the house and he worried about the inconvenience to his family. As was so often the case, FDR had his thumb squarely on the pulse of the nation and his predictions proved accurate, if somewhat understated. Enormous public interest brought over 500,000 people a year to the site in the late 1940s and early 50s. Over 100,000 people came in August 1949 alone, and on a single day in October 1947, 10,000 people filed past FDR's grave.[2]

FDR's gift to the United States included the "Big House," the estate buildings, gravesite and thirty-three acres of land adjoining the Library property and Albany Post Road (Rte. 9). Clearly, he envisioned the two Presidential gifts, the Library and the Home, together and planned that they would serve the public in a complementary way. Curiously, he did not build in protection for the view from the home of his beloved Hudson River. His estate provided no long-term protective measures for Val-Kill or his cottage retreat on Dutchess Hill. Nor did he set up any permanent protection for the majority of the nearly 1400-acre family estate, his life-long home and presidential refuge where he indulged his passion for the land through a variety of reforestation and farm programs.

FDR assumed, mistakenly, that his family would want to continue living on the property over the long-term and in doing so would serve, de facto, as stewards of the property. By 1970, when the last Roosevelt family land ownership in Hyde Park ended, the estate was a far different place than it was in 1946. Since its dedication, the Roosevelt Home has stood as a silent witness to the transformation of the surrounding area from a rural landscape characterized by farms and forests to a suburban landscape of commercial and residential development.

The family inherited a life estate at the "Big House," which Eleanor Roosevelt gave up immediately after it opened to the public. Through the terms of FDR's will, the rest of the property was distributed by the estate trustees. The Roosevelts' second son, Elliott Roosevelt, acquired the largest portion, particularly the lands east of the Albany Post Road. As early as 1949, Elliott began the transformation of the east side of the Post Road by leasing or selling parcels for a variety of commercial and residential uses, including a service station, a Howard Johnson's restaurant, the Hyde Park Gift Shop and a residential development. In the early 1950s, housing sprang up along Violet Avenue (Rte. 9G), and the largest housing developments occurred at the northeastern reaches of the estate, beyond Val-Kill.

For a brief time Elliott carried on the estate agricultural tradition by setting up and operating Val-Kill Farms. He successfully harvested 50,000 trees for the 1946 Christmas season, but by 1952 he gave up the marginal farm operation and sold that property. Further business development, including construction of a shopping mall, took place in the mid-1950s on the southwestern portion of the estate, property that FDR had inherited from his half-brother, James R. ("Rosy") Roosevelt.

Then, in the 1970s alarm bells sounded over a development threat to the historic core of Val-Kill, and spurred the intervention of several major efforts that would turn the tide toward protecting the remaining estate lands.

In 1952, the Franklin D. Roosevelt Foundation (later the Franklin and Eleanor Roosevelt Institute) purchased and donated to the National Park Service the acreage between the Roosevelt Home and the Hudson River, thus securing the view and the river setting of the home. A major gift from the heir to the neighboring Newbold estate, Gerald Morgan, further secured the river lands on the north.

The Val-Kill complex and 170 surrounding acres were saved

through an impressive grassroots effort by a Dutchess County group that later became the Eleanor Roosevelt Center at Val-Kill. As a result of their work and advocacy with Congress, Val-Kill opened to the public as a National Historic Site in 1984, the 100th anniversary of Eleanor Roosevelt's birth.

In 1996, the Open Space Institute purchased Top Cottage. They also bought the southernmost Hudson River parcel of the estate, and another parcel bordering Val-Kill. Top Cottage and its landscape were carefully restored to FDR's design by the Franklin and Eleanor Roosevelt Institute and opened to the public in 2001 as part of the Home of FDR National Historic Site.

In 1998, Congress buoyed up the estate's future with legislation enabling the National Park Service to purchase property within the historic boundary. When the Red House (James Roosevelt's home) went on the market in 2001, the Roosevelt Institute again stepped in, buying and restoring much of the building's historic appearance.

Recently, Scenic Hudson has purchased key parcels fronting on Albany Post Road, including the 1949 drive-in property and the major 334-acre parcel connecting the estate lands between the Post Road and Violet Avenue. Here a public/private effort is underway to develop an agricultural-theme operation carefully designed to both promote tourism and protect and enhance FDR's forest plantations.[3]

Still other organizations, the Hyde Park Corridor Committee and the Hyde Park Trail Committee are active in planning for the Post Road/Rte. 9 corridor and new recreational uses of the area. Another group, Honoring Eleanor Roosevelt: Preserving Her Val-Kill Home, is raising funds to overhaul the exhibits and general visitor experience at Val-Kill.

The Henry A. Wallace Visitor and Education Center carries on a three decades-long history of private and public efforts conducted on behalf of the Roosevelts' Hyde Park legacy. When the Wallace Center opened in November 2003, a partnership of the National Archives and Records Administration, the National Park Service and the Franklin and Eleanor Roosevelt Institute accomplished an important leap in its goal to reinvigorate the way people visit the Roosevelt Home and Library. The stunning new facility, which resonates with the Dutch Colonial design ethic that FDR loved, sits on the historic Newbold property where it provides an ideal starting point from which to visit the Home, Library, Gravesite and surrounding landscape.

Spring 2005 now approaches and the graves of Franklin and Eleanor Roosevelt and their dog, Fala, are still snow-covered. FDR would have difficulty recognizing today's visitors who belong to a different world than his, but a world that in so many ways he defined. He might recognize, however, treasured pieces of his Hyde Park estate and would surely relish the many new ways people can explore the legacy of his property.

NOTES

[1] *The New York Times*, April 13, 1946.

[2] Draft: Administrative History, Roosevelt-Vanderbilt National Historic Sites, Jann Warren-Findley, 2005.

[3] The history of the Roosevelt estate is detailed in John Auwaerter's "Roosevelt Estate Historic Resource Study," Part III, (draft), July 2004.

Index